THE CAMBRIDGE BIBLE COMMENTARY

NEW ENGLISH BIBLE

GENERAL EDITORS
P. R. ACKROYD, A. R. C. LEANEY
J. W. PACKER

DANIEL

THE BOOK OF
DANIEL

COMMENTARY BY

RAYMOND HAMMER

Lecturer in Theology, The Queen's College, Birmingham

CAMBRIDGE UNIVERSITY PRESS

CAMBRIDGE

LONDON · NEW YORK · MELBOURNE

Published by the Syndics of the Cambridge University Press
The Pitt Building, Trumpington Street, Cambridge CB2 1RP
Bentley House, 200 Euston Road, London NW1 2DB
32 East 57th Street, New York, NY 10022, USA
296 Beaconsfield Parade, Middle Park, Melbourne 3206, Australia

First published 1976

Printed in Great Britain
at the
University Printing House, Cambridge
(Harry Myers, University Printer)

Library of Congress cataloguing in publication data
Bible. O.T. Daniel. English. New English. 1976.
The Book of Daniel.
(The Cambridge Bible commentary, New English Bible)
Bibliography: p.
Includes index.
I. Bible. O.T. Daniel – Commentaries. I. Hammer,
Raymond. II. Title. III. Series.
BS1553.H35   224′.5′077   76–4241
ISBN 0 521 08654 X hard covers
ISBN 0 521 09765 7 paperback

GENERAL EDITORS' PREFACE

The aim of this series is to provide the text of the New English Bible closely linked to a commentary in which the results of modern scholarship are made available to the general reader. Teachers and young people have been especially kept in mind. The commentators have been asked to assume no specialized theological knowledge, and no knowledge of Greek and Hebrew. Bare references to other literature and multiple references to other parts of the Bible have been avoided. Actual quotations have been given as often as possible.

The completion of the New Testament part of the series in 1967 provides a basis upon which the production of the much larger Old Testament and Apocrypha series can be undertaken. The welcome accorded to the series has been an encouragement to the editors to follow the same general pattern, and an attempt has been made to take account of criticisms which have been offered. One necessary change is the inclusion of the translators' footnotes since in the Old Testament these are more extensive, and essential for the understanding of the text.

Within the severe limits imposed by the size and scope of the series, each commentator will attempt to set out the main findings of recent biblical scholarship and to describe the historical background to the text. The main theological issues will also be critically discussed.

Much attention has been given to the form of the volumes. The aim is to produce books each of which will be read consecutively from first to last page. The introductory material leads naturally into the text, which itself leads into the alternating sections of the commentary.

The series is accompanied by three volumes of a more general character. *Understanding the Old Testament* sets out to provide the larger historical and archaeological background, to say something about the life and thought of the people of the Old Testament, and to answer the question 'Why should we study the Old Testament?'. *The Making of the Old Testament* is concerned with the formation of the books of the Old Testament and Apocrypha in the context of the ancient near eastern world, and with the ways in which these books have come down to us in the life of the Jewish and Christian communities. *Old Testament Illustrations* contains maps, diagrams and photographs with an explanatory text. These three volumes are designed to provide material helpful to the understanding of the individual books and their commentaries, but they are also prepared so as to be of use quite independently.

P. R. A.
A. R. C. L.
J. W. P.

CONTENTS

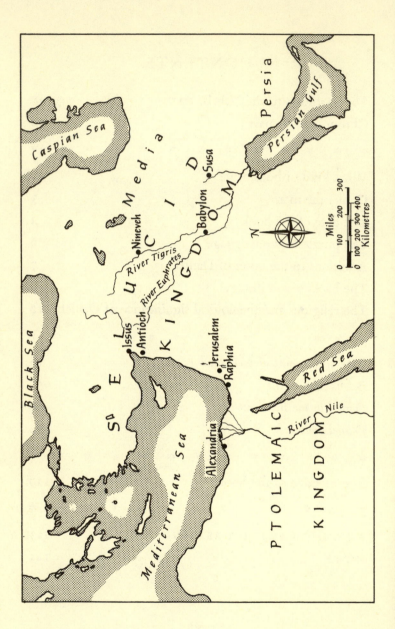

THE FOOTNOTES TO THE
N.E.B. TEXT

The footnotes to the N.E.B. text are designed to help the reader either to understand particular points of detail – the meaning of a name, the presence of a play upon words – or to give information about the actual text. Where the Hebrew text appears to be erroneous, or there is doubt about its precise meaning, it may be necessary to turn to manuscripts which offer a different wording, or to ancient translations of the text which may suggest a better reading, or to offer a new explanation based upon conjecture. In such cases, the footnotes supply very briefly an indication of the evidence, and whether the solution proposed is one that is regarded as possible or as probable. Various abbreviations are used in the footnotes:

(1) Some abbreviations are simply of terms used in explaining a point: *ch(s).*, chapter(s); *cp.*, compare; *lit.*, literally; *mng.*, meaning; *MS(S).*, manuscript(s), i.e. Hebrew manuscript(s), unless otherwise stated; *om.*, omit(s); *or*, indicating an alternative interpretation; *poss.*, possible; *prob.*, probable; *rdg.*, reading; *Vs(s).*, version(s).

(2) Other abbreviations indicate sources of information from which better interpretations or readings may be obtained.

Aq. Aquila, a Greek translator of the Old Testament (perhaps about A.D. 130) characterized by great literalness.

Aram. Aramaic – may refer to the text in this language (used in parts of Ezra and Daniel), or to the meaning of an Aramaic word. Aramaic belongs to the same language family as Hebrew, and is known from about 1000 B.C. over a wide area of the Middle East, including Palestine.

Heb. Hebrew – may refer to the Hebrew text or may indicate the literal meaning of the Hebrew word.

Josephus Flavius Josephus (A.D. 37/8–about 100), author of the *Jewish Antiquities*, a survey of the whole history of his people, directed partly at least to a non-Jewish audience, and of various other works, notably one on the *Jewish War* (that of A.D. 66–73) and a defence of Judaism (*Against Apion*).

Luc. Sept. Lucian's recension of the Septuagint, an important edition made in Antioch in Syria about the end of the third century A.D.

Pesh. Peshitta or Peshitto, the Syriac version of the Old Testament. Syriac is the name given chiefly to a form of Eastern Aramaic used by the Christian community. The translation varies in quality, and is at many points influenced by the Septuagint or the Targums.

Sam.   Samaritan Pentateuch – the form of the first five books of the Old Testament as used by the Samaritan community. It is written in Hebrew in a special form of the Old Hebrew script, and preserves an important form of the text, somewhat influenced by Samaritan ideas.

Scroll(s)   Scroll(s), commonly called the Dead Sea Scrolls, found at or near Qumran from 1947 onwards. These important manuscripts shed light on the state of the Hebrew text as it was developing in the last centuries B.C. and the first century A.D.

Sept.   Septuagint (meaning 'seventy'; often abbreviated as the Roman numeral LXX), the name given to the main Greek version of the Old Testament. According to tradition, the Pentateuch was translated in Egypt in the third century B.C. by 70 (or 72) translators, six from each tribe, but the precise nature of its origin and development is not fully known. It was intended to provide Greek-speaking Jews with a convenient translation. Subsequently it came to be much revered by the Christian community.

Symm.   Symmachus, another Greek translator of the Old Testament (beginning of the third century A.D.), who tried to combine literalness with good style. Both Lucian and Jerome viewed his version with favour.

Targ.   Targum, a name given to various Aramaic versions of the Old Testament, produced over a long period and eventually standardized, for the use of Aramaic-speaking Jews.

Theod.   Theodotion,the author of a revision of the Septuagint (probably second century A.D.), very dependent on the Hebrew text.

Vulg.   Vulgate, the most important Latin version of the Old Testament, produced by Jerome about A.D. 400, and the text most used throughout the Middle Ages in western Christianity.

[. . .]   In the text itself square brackets are used to indicate probably late additions to the Hebrew text.

(Fuller discussion of a number of these points may be found in *The Making of the Old Testament* in this series)

CHRONOLOGICAL CHART

BABYLONIAN EMPIRE

Nabopolassar (625–605 B.C.)

Nebuchadnezzar (604–561 B.C.) (chs. 1–4; 7: 4)

Amel-Marduk (561–559 B.C.) (murdered) (called Evil-
    Merodach in 2 Kings 25: 27)
Nergal-Sharezar (559–556 B.C.) (brother-in-law of Amel-
    Marduk) (possibly to be identified with
    King Neriglissar, mentioned by the
    historian Berosus)
Labushi-Marduk (556–555 B.C.) (murdered)

Nabonidus (Nabuna'id) (555–538 B.C.)

Belshazzar (not king, but regent for his father) (ch. 5;
    7:1; 8: 1)

PERSIAN EMPIRE (2: 39; 7: 5; 8: 3–4)

Cyrus (558–529 B.C.) (1: 21; 10: 1; 11: 2)
    (He was first king of Anshan; conquered Media
    about 550 B.C., became king of Persia about
    547 B.C., and conquered Babylon in 538 B.C.)
Cambyses (529–521 B.C.)

Darius I (521–486 B.C.)

Xerxes (= Ahasuerus in the Old Testament) (485–465 B.C.)
      (9: 1f; 11: 2)
Artaxerxes I (465–424 B.C.)

[continued on page xii

PERSIAN EMPIRE (*cont.*)

Darius II (423–404 B.C.)
|
Artaxerxes II (404–359 B.C.)
|
Artaxerxes III (359–338 B.C.)
|
Darius III (336–331 B.C.)
(conquered by Alexander in 331 B.C.)

GREEK KINGDOMS (2: 40; 7: 7)

Alexander the Great (336–323 B.C.) (8: 5–8; 11: 3–4)
The Ptolemies
Ptolemy I (323*–285 B.C.)
Ptolemy II (285–246 B.C.)
Ptolemy III (246–221 B.C.)
Ptolemy IV (221–203 B.C.)
Ptolemy V (203–181 B.C.)
Ptolemy VI (181–145 B.C.)

* He became satrap of Egypt in 323 B.C. and king in 305 B.C.

The Seleucids
Seleucus I (312–280 B.C.) (11: 5)
Antiochus I (280–261 B.C.) (11: 6)
Antiochus II (261–247 B.C.) (11: 6)
Seleucus II (247–226 B.C.) (11: 7)
Seleucus III (226–223 B.C.)
Antiochus III (the Great) (223–187 B.C.) (11: 10–19)
Seleucus IV (187–175 B.C.) (11: 20)
Antiochus IV (Epiphanes) (175–164 B.C.) (7: 8, 11, 20;
8: 9, 23; 11: 21–45)

THE BOOK OF
DANIEL

✳ ✳ ✳ ✳ ✳ ✳ ✳ ✳ ✳ ✳ ✳ ✳ ✳

WHAT KIND OF BOOK IS IT?

In the English Bible, the book of Daniel occupies a place after the major prophets (Isaiah, Jeremiah and Ezekiel), a position that it received in the Septuagint, the Greek translation of the Old Testament. The earliest manuscripts and fragments of the book come from the caves near the Dead Sea, where discoveries were made from 1947 onwards, now known as the Dead Sea Scrolls. The caves held what amounts to a library belonging to a Jewish community based on Qumran. One fragment from the fourth cave uses the title 'Daniel the prophet' and this is also the title used in Matt. 24: 15. In the Hebrew Bible, however, the book is not included amongst the prophetic writings. The Hebrew canon consists of three divisions, the 'Law', the 'Prophets' and the 'Writings', and Daniel is included in the third and last division. This suggests that the book was not known by 200 B.C., about the time when the collection of prophetic writings was assembled. Ecclesiasticus in the Apocrypha (a book which is dated about 180 B.C.) refers to the saints and heroes of the past, drawing upon most of the Old Testament for its material, but makes no reference to Daniel. We can only suppose that the book was not known to the writer of Ecclesiasticus. We have evidence, however, that the book was known and revered from the middle of the second century B.C. The Sibylline Oracles (a collection of prophecies and wise sayings, drawn from pagan, Jewish and Christian sources which date from about 500 B.C. to 400 A.D.) contains quotations from the book of Daniel in a section commonly dated to the middle of the second century B.C. The book of Daniel was also popular with the Qumran community whose library dates from early in the second century B.C. onwards.

The question 'What kind of book is it?' still remains to be answered. A cursory look at the book tells us that there are two definite sections, in the first of which we have a series of stories, in which pious Jews are depicted as challenging worldly power, whilst the second claims to be a series of visions granted by God to Daniel. The stories are told *about* Daniel and his companions, whilst the visions are given in the first person. The first section seems to be concerned with the historical, in which God's action or intervention is seen as crucial, if the faithful are to be vindicated and God's control of human affairs to be universally acknowledged; the second section sees history as moving inevitably to its divinely determined goal.

As we shall see when we look at the religious and theological emphases in the book, there is much which links it in spirit with the prophetic books. Many scholars, however, would think of Daniel as the first great Jewish apocalyptic writing. There exists a large number of later writings which were not accepted as canonical, all of which claim to be apocalypses (or revelations) given by God to some ancient 'man of God', which are then relevant for the age in which the books were written. They are all pseudonymous – i.e. they profess to be written by the ancient seers, although it is quite impossible to regard them as such. (The book of Revelation shows parallels with this literature, but has as its professed author a 'John' who is likely to be the actual author rather than a figure of the past.)

The second section of Daniel can also be said to be pseudonymous, for, as we shall see, it is most improbable that it was the work of a sixth-century B.C. Jewish exile, which the first section claims Daniel to be. It is also apocalyptic in the sense that it claims to disclose or reveal what is known to God, but hidden from man's general understanding. There is also an extensive use of symbols and fantastic figures, such as we already have in the prophet Ezekiel.

DANIEL THE MAN

The book of Daniel begins by telling us that Daniel, together with his three friends, Shadrach, Meshach and Abed-nego, was amongst the Jews who were taken captive at the fall of Jerusalem (606 B.C. according to the chronology of the book) and brought to Babylon. Elsewhere in the Old Testament, however, we have no mention of a Daniel during the period of the Babylonian exile. In the prophet Ezekiel a Danel (or Daniel) occurs alongside Noah and Job (14: 14, 20), all three being examples of righteous men. Ezekiel later refers to him as an exceptionally wise person (28: 3). Both passages suggest that he belongs to the dim and distant past. Outside the Old Testament there is reference to a king by the name of Daniel or Dan'el in the Ugaritic literature, discovered at Ras Shamra (in northern Palestine) in the 1930s, which is usually dated about the fourteenth century B.C. Daniel (or Dan'el) is also noted there for his righteousness and wisdom, and it is likely that Ezekiel drew upon ancient Canaanite legends, when he gave Daniel as his example of uprightness and wisdom.

As the book of Daniel appears to be indebted to Ezekiel for much of its imagery, it is possible that the writer uses the name of this ancient figure to indicate the role that the 'righteous' and 'wise' Jew would play in the crisis, in which he finds himself. As we shall see, the crisis belongs not to the period of the exile but to the second century B.C., and it is to that time that we should date the book.

THE DATE OF THE BOOK

As has been indicated, the first section of the book appears to tell the story of Daniel and his friends in Babylon during the period of the exile in the sixth century B.C. The second section also claims to be a series of visions belonging to the same period, and the history which is contained in them goes from the Babylonian period to the second century B.C. There are, however, a number of historical problems raised by the writings.

One would expect a writer in the sixth century B.C. to be reasonably accurate on major historical events, but such is not the case. Belshazzar is represented as the son of Nebuchadnezzar (Dan. 5: 11), although he was the son of Nabonidus (Nabuna'id). He was heir to the throne and may have acted as regent in his father's absence, but he was never actually king (despite Dan. 5: 1–30; 8: 1). The book also regards 'Darius the Mede' (Dan. 5: 31; 6: 28) as responsible for the conquest of Babylon and its first ruler. Persian records refer to the conquest by Cyrus and to the governorship of Gubaru (Gobryas), a Persian. The word 'Chaldaeans' (Dan. 2: 2, etc.) is used to describe an astrologer, but was not used in this way in the sixth century B.C. It is unlikely that Daniel would have had a prefectship over the astrologers (Dan. 2: 48), as this would have involved membership of the Babylonian priesthood. (Nehemiah and Esther both refer, however, to high positions held by Jews at the *Persian* court.)

In fact the book is far better informed about the period 300–165 B.C. than about the period of the exile, in which the stories and visions are set. For example, ch. 11 makes brief reference to the Persian period (only four kings being mentioned) and to Alexander the Great, but interest is largely concentrated upon Greek rule in Palestine. Here, there is a remarkable agreement with Greek historical writings of the period, and the record brings us to the period after Antiochus IV Epiphanes, the Seleucid ruler, had desecrated the Jewish

4

temple in Jerusalem. There are numerous references to this happening in 168 B.C. (see Dan. 7: 25; 8: 14; 9: 17; 12: 7) and the attempts to suppress Judaism. Dan. 11: 45 anticipates the death of Antiochus (which occurred in 164 B.C.), but there is no precise reference to it. It is as though the strictly historical comes to an end just before the rededication of the temple and the subsequent death of Antiochus. In place of strictly historical narrative we have the expectation that there will be only a brief interval before the end comes (7: 25; 9: 27). The survey of history in 11: 1–39 moves into prophetic prediction in 11: 40 – 12: 3. The precise moment of the end is still seen as open to doubt and subsequent revision (12: 11–12). As we have no reference to the recapure of Jerusalem by the forces of Judas Maccabaeus or to the rededication of the temple, and no knowledge of Antiochus' futile expedition to the east, it is likely that the book, as we now have it, was completed by 165 B.C. The fact that the book is not included in the prophetic canon (completed about 200 B.C.) or mentioned in Ecclesiasticus (about 180 B.C.) further supports this date in the second century B.C. A look at the actual text also supports this later date. The Hebrew style resembles that of Chronicles, Esther and Ecclesiastes (all later books), and there is a higher number of Persian and Greek loan-words than in other books of the Old Testament. For example, the word *raz* comes from the Persian, and is used to express the idea of a 'secret' or 'mystery' (Dan. 2: 18; 4: 9), whilst the word *sumphonyah* translated as 'music' in the N.E.B. (Dan. 3: 5, 10, 15) is Greek in origin and appears to have been used of a musical instrument only from the second century B.C. (The Revised Standard Version translates it as 'bagpipe', but it is more likely to have been a stringed instrument, as it is listed with other string instruments.)

We have spoken of 'the book, as we now have it', and this expression leaves open the possibility (or even the probability) that the stories in the first part of the book were already well known before their incorporation into the book and adaptation to the main message of the writer. Many writers, for example, point to the much better relationship between Jews and the pagan rulers shown in the stories than could have been possible at the time when the book was issued in the reign of Antiochus IV Epiphanes. The stories, whilst emphasizing that pagan rulers need to acknowledge that God alone is ultimately in control of human affairs, reflect the more liberal attitude of the third century B.C., when Jews were ready to assimilate a great amount of Greek culture.

THE PUZZLE OF THE LANGUAGE

The book of Daniel, as we have it, is written in two languages. It begins in Hebrew, but changes to Aramaic at 2: 4. The Aramaic continues to the end of ch. 7, but the last five chapters are all written once again in Hebrew. The fact that this mixed character of the book goes right back to early copies is now known through the discovery of the Dead Sea Scrolls. The earliest portions of Daniel, which come from Caves I and IV, indicate these changes from Hebrew to Aramaic at 2: 4 and back from Aramaic to Hebrew at 8: 1. On the assumption that the book is a unity, some have assumed that it was originally written in Aramaic and that parts were subsequently translated into Hebrew. It is suggested that the book would not have been accepted without a Hebrew introduction. Aramaic was the language of trade throughout the Fertile Crescent, but the assumption that it would have been spoken in Babylon is mistaken. Some suggest that, whereas the stories were originally written in Aramaic, the visions were written in Hebrew, and that a subsequent editor translated the opening section into Hebrew and the first vision into Aramaic, in order to stress identity between the two sections. Another suggestion is that the original chapters were issued separately in the vernacular, but that the later chapters were written in Hebrew to emphasize their religious significance.

It is possible that the author drew upon a number of earlier stories, to which ch. 7 was added as an interpretation. There is a close link between ch. 7 and ch. 2. Subsequently the same writer, or possibly his disciple, recorded the visions in the last five chapters as a kind of commentary on, or expansion of, the dream in ch. 7.

The fact that so many suggestions have been made to explain the text is itself an indication of the uncertainty attaching to any theory. In attempting to answer the question whether the authorship is single or composite we shall need to look at the contents rather than at the language. Whilst some would point to the overall theological unity and the attempt to keep the exile as the setting for the whole book, there are some fundamental differences of approach which suggest that the first part of the book contains older traditions which have been written to fit a second-century context, but where the original ethos has been largely preserved. In the visions there is a very decided dualism, and Antiochus, in particular, shows no saving graces. By contrast, in the legends, Nebuchadnezzer, Belshazzar and Darius, in turn, are all represented as acknowledging that knowledge and authority really belong to God. Despite the story of the furnace in ch. 3, the chapters show a fairly lenient attitude towards the Jewish captives, which would suit either the Persian period or early in the Greek period, as we have already suggested.

ADDITIONS TO THE BOOK OF DANIEL

A comparison between the text of the book of Daniel in the Hebrew Old Testament and that preserved in two separate Greek versions (the Septuagint and that made by Theodotion, a proselyte from Ephesus, in the middle of the second century A.D.) shows that several additions were made to the text of Daniel. The most important are to be found in the Apocrypha, consisting of the 'Song of the Three' (inserted into the story of the blazing furnace in ch. 3), 'Daniel and Susanna' and 'Daniel, Bel, and the Snake' (both appended to the book, as we have it in the Old Testament). For the relationship of these writings to the canonical book of Daniel, reference should be made to *The Shorter Books of the Apocrypha* in this series.

THE BACKGROUND HISTORY

Although we have decided to date the book in the second century B.C., it contains references to the period from the fall of Jerusalem (586 B.C.) to the year before the death of Antiochus IV Epiphanes (i.e. 165 B.C.). Nebuchadnezzar, although the second king in the new Babylonian Empire which came into prominence after the collapse of Assyria with the fall of Nineveh in 612 B.C., was responsible for its greatest expansion. Already in 605 B.C. (before he became king) Nebuchadnezzar had overthrown Egypt at the great battle of Carchemish. He was renowned for his wealth and grandeur, and it is understandable that he should be identified with the gold of the image in ch. 2. The hanging gardens of Babylon were remembered in later generations and numbered among the wonders of the ancient world. His immediate successors did not reign for long, and the last king Nabonidus (or Nabuna'id) (555–538 B.C.) was not a relative, although it has been suggested that he married a widow of Nebuchadnezzar, and that his son Belshazzar is accordingly called the son of Nebuchadnezzar in ch. 5.

The book of Daniel supposes that the Babylonian Empire was succeeded by a Median Empire. Darius the Mede is described as a son of Ahasuerus (= Xerxes) (9: 1) and as the successor to Belshazzar on the conquest of Babylon (5: 31). It seems to be implied in 6: 28 that Darius gave place to Cyrus the Persian. In actual fact Babylonian power was replaced by *Persian*, for Cyrus, who had begun as king of Anshan in 558 B.C. and conquered Media in 550 B.C., became king of the Medes and Persians in 547 B.C. and was the conqueror of Babylon in 538 B.C. It is possible that the author of Daniel was influenced by the older prophets who had lived in an earlier day, when Media rather than Persia was the power involved in overthrowing Assyria and posing a threat to Babylon (e.g. Isa. 13: 17; Jer. 51: 11). It is likely that the name Darius was taken from Darius I (king of Persia from 521 to 486 B.C.), who was responsible for the division of the empire into satrapies (or provinces). (Whilst 6: 1 speaks of Darius establishing 120 satrapies, in actual fact the area of the satrapy was very much greater and the Greek historian Herodotus refers to 'twenty'.) The fact that, historically, we must think of one Medo-Persian Empire rather than of two separate kingdoms is reflected in the vision of the 'ram with two horns' (8: 3). There is, however, a link between Darius I and Babylon, because, early in his reign, he was forced to put down a revolt in Babylon, where a supposed son of Nabonidus made a bid for independence. The prophet Haggai (2: 22) refers to these disturbances at the beginning of the reign of Darius, and it is possible that Darius, rather than Cyrus, was associated in the mind of the writer of Daniel with the fall of Babylon and the subsequent return of the exiles to Jerusalem because Haggai was regarded as one of the prophets at the return.

The Persian Empire continued for over 200 years, and it was largely a time of peace for the Jews. Accordingly Jewish history makes little of the period, referring simply to some of the most important rulers. For the Jews the consolidation of their religion and customs in this period was the most important issue.

Alexander the Great succeeded his father Philip as king of Macedon in 336 B.C. and in a series of campaigns from 334 B.C. crushed Persian power and spread his control to the Indus valley. The book of Daniel refers to the lightning advance of his forces (8: 5–8) and to his sudden death in 323 B.C. (11: 3–4) before he had achieved his aim of combining Greek ideals with Egyptian and Asian traditions. The kingdom of Macedon fell into the hands of his general Antigonus, whilst two other of his generals, Ptolemy and Seleucus, shared out most of his Asian empire. Ptolemy and his successors, based on the newly-built city of Alexandria (founded in 332 B.C.) in Egypt, controlled Palestine (see 11: 5) for over 100 years. There was continuing rivalry between the Seleucid rulers (called 'kings of the north' in Daniel) and the Ptolemies (called 'kings of the south') despite attempts at alliance through marriage (see 11: 6). In 217 B.C. the Seleucid ruler, Antiochus III (called 'the Great'), swept south, occupying Palestine and threatening Egypt. By 202 B.C. he had consolidated his control over Palestine and, despite attempts at reconquest on the part of Egypt, Seleucid rule persisted. A clash with Rome prevented further expansion of Seleucid power, and Antiochus III was forced to hand over his younger son (the future Antiochus IV Epiphanes) as a hostage.

The Jews had enjoyed a fairly easy time under the rule of the Ptolemies and had already absorbed a great deal of Greek culture, and, initially, Seleucid domination still permitted religious freedom and a certain measure of local autonomy under the high priest in Jerusalem. The wars of Antiochus III, however, had left the Seleucid Empire almost bankrupt, and his successor, Seleucus IV, attempted to seize the temple treasures (see 11: 20). In 177 B.C., by which time his younger brother Antiochus had been hostage in Rome for twelve years, Demetrius, his son, replaced him as hostage, and Antiochus moved to Athens. When Seleucus IV was murdered by Heliodorus, Antiochus managed to seize control (175 B.C.) and became king as Antiochus IV (see 7: 8; 8: 9; 11: 21).

The stage was now set for a fierce challenge to Jewish religious and social practices, and within Judaism there was a divide between the party of the *Hasidim*, supported by Onias III, the high priest, who stood for a strict observance of the Law and loyalty to the past, and the liberalizing group who sought for close assimilation to Greek ideals and practice. Antiochus IV, like his elder brother Seleucus IV, was financially embarrassed and sought to plunder temple treasures, whenever possible. Jason, the brother of Onias III, was appointed as high priest as a more likely collaborator, but in 171 B.C. he

was, in turn, replaced by Menelaus, and Onias was murdered
(see 9 : 26; 11 : 22). In his first invasion of Egypt Antiochus
met with success (170 B.C.), but, on his second expedition in
169 B.C., he was forced to turn back by the Roman legate and
made to renounce any claim to Egypt. On his return north
the previous year Antiochus had plundered the Jerusalem
temple and massacred many Jews, because Jason had tried to
reinstate himself as high priest, but now, thwarted by the
Romans in his imperialist desires, he vented his wrath upon
the Jews. The king had desired to unify his empire by a policy
of hellenization and from 169 B.C. his coinage incorporated
the claim that he was the visible representative of the Most
High God. Naturally the Jews were seen as the great stumbl-
ing-block to unification of culture and religion. Jerusalem
was seized on the Sabbath day, many Jews massacred or
driven into exile, and orders came for the complete suppression
of the Jewish religion. Circumcision and other customs were
forbidden and sabbath observance prohibited. The scrolls of
the Law were burnt, the temple daily sacrifices abolished and
a heathen altar set up in the temple on the 15th day of Kislev
(December) 168 B.C. (As we shall see the book of Daniel
makes many references to these events.)

Whilst most of the *Hasidim* responded with passive resistance, Mattathias and his sons raised the standard of revolt, and
one son Judas, nicknamed 'the Hammer' (Maccabaeus),
succeeded in recovering Jerusalem after a series of battles,
although, for a time, the Seleucid garrison remained in the
citadel. On the 25th day of Kislev (i.e. in December) 165 B.C. the
temple was cleansed and rededicated. In the meantime,
Antiochus himself had been campaigning further east, largely in
search of more money. He tried to pillage a temple at Elymais
in Persia, but was beaten off by the town's inhabitants, and
soon afterwards (in 164 B.C.) he died at Taboe, another Persian
town. This event, however, takes us beyond the scope of the
book, for, as we have seen, whilst the death of Antiochus was
anticipated as part of God's judgement on human attempts at

self-deification and self-glorification, the book was put out before the rededication of the temple.

For the history of the Jewish persecution under Antiochus IV Epiphanes reference should be made to the First and Second Books of the Maccabees, to be found in the Apocrypha. The First Book is by far the more important of the two, as it gives a minute account of Jewish history from the accession of Antiochus Epiphanes in 175 B.C. to the death of Simon (brother of Judas Maccabaeus) in 135 B.C. The different aspects of the religious persecution and the desecration of the temple are described in 1 Macc. 1: 41–64, whilst 1 Macc. 4: 36–59 tells of the purification of the temple and the rededication of the altar for Jewish sacrifices. The Second Book of the Maccabees was written a little later (about 124 B.C.) and covers the period from 176 B.C. to 161 B.C. Most regard it as a less reliable source than the First Book. Both books survive in the Greek Old Testament, but it is commonly thought that the First Book was originally written in Hebrew. (There are two further books of the Maccabees in most Septuagint manuscripts, but they are much later compositions and have no value for the study of the book of Daniel.)

THE RELIGIOUS AND THEOLOGICAL SIGNIFICANCE OF DANIEL

At the time when the stories about Daniel and his friends and the visions were brought together, genuine prophecy had come to an end and it was difficult for anyone to claim that he had a message from God for the times. The fact that the Septuagint (the Greek translation of the Old Testament) places Daniel with the prophets is an indication that Jews came to see its message as continuous with that of the prophets. Many, however, see the book as the first apocalyptic writing – not because there can be said to be a special class of literature by that name, but because many of the features of Daniel were taken over by subsequent writers who also claimed to be disclosing the hidden goal of history, as they uncovered and reinterpreted the meaning of the historic events through which they had been passing. At the same time there was an attempt to indicate the relevance of older Hebrew prophecy for the later age in which they were living. Like Daniel, they looked for some hero of the past as the 'author' of the message they were putting forth. The hero chosen as the supposed author often had a link with the message, and the name Daniel ('God is my judge') itself spoke of God's wisdom in judgement – a theme which marks the book as a whole.

In the apocalyptic message the idea of a coming world crisis was given increased prominence; it is seen as the culmination of history. The human attempts at grandeur, typified by the four empires (ch. 2), are swept aside. Man may set up his own gods and demand that they alone be worshipped (ch. 3), but God can protect those who trust in him, and even if the faithful meet with martyrdom God is able to resurrect them to new life (ch. 12). Human empires can in themselves only express the bestial (chs. 4 and 7), but the human figure, the source of true authority with whom the destiny of the 'saints of the Most High' is to be identified, comes down from heaven. The writer sees Antiochus Epiphanes (whose name itself claims that he is the manifestation on earth of Zeus) as the embodiment of all that opposes the divine will. He may vaunt himself and seek to overthrow the faith, but he, in turn, will be destroyed. As the little horn (7: 8), he is the end of the historical process, but history has no meaning apart from God. He is no longer Epiphanes (the (god) manifest), but Epimanes (the madman), for there can be no true wisdom and knowledge apart from God. It is madness to live and act as though one were oneself divine.

But the book of Daniel, as a tract for the times, says something about the life of faith. The Psalms had depicted the 'man of loyalty' who was true to the covenant which God had established with his people, whilst the prophet Hosea had written of God's own faithfulness to the commitments he had made in forging the covenant with Israel. Now Daniel writes of the men loyal to the Law of God, those who refuse to compromise and who remain steadfast to the point of death. The supreme point of history is almost immediately upon them. With the end at hand – an end which was to usher in the universally acknowledged rule of God – the faithful were to live in hope and expectancy.

But history is to be caught up in supra-history, and so the truth of the age to come can only be communicated through images and symbols. Already the prophet Ezekiel had made lavish use of symbolic animal imagery, and this practice is continued in Daniel. It is no novelty; the language of myth is once again used to convey the truth about God's determining hand in history. Nations have their heavenly representatives among the angelic forces, and there is but a short step to the point where the New Testament Apocalypse (the book of Revelation) is to describe conflict on earth in terms of a heavenly conflict. The experience of persecution itself leads to the intensive polarizing between the divine forces for good and the forces for evil which meet ultimately with destruction. Power which has emerged from the primal chaos cannot but return to the chaos of destruction. God who creates a cosmos (= world order) can alone give meaning. Knowledge is his prerogative, and it is only as recipients of the divine gift that men can be wise. It is because the saving blessings of the coming age are already pre-existent in the heavenly sphere that they can descend from there to the earth (ch. 7: 13). By placing the setting in the age of the exile, the writer is able to look at his present and immediate future as events predetermined by God in the past. The theological truth that this device communicates is that all rests within the divine will. That is why prediction becomes a possibility. It is no longer simply the case of a prophet overhearing or looking in on the divine counsel; a revelation from God is communicated to Daniel. He may need to keep it secret, but it can be divulged when it is relevant. If its fulfilment still lies in the future, the secret cannot be fully understood (8: 26–7). It is only the 'wise' who can decode the 'mystery' and give the true 'interpretation', and it is at this point that Daniel is seen as the heir of all the 'wise'. There is the succession of wisdom as well as the succession of the *Ḥasidim* (the pious ones). Whereas there had been a certain openness in traditional prophecy, we are now confronted with a hiddenness within the revelation. Because 'interpretation' is necessary, it is possible to find 'reinterpretation', where a later writer claims to be the recipient of a new understanding of the divine truth. Daniel can reinterpret Jeremiah (9: 2–19), but the writer of 2 Esdras will later claim the right to reinterpret Daniel (compare 2 Esdras 12: 11 with Dan. 7: 7) and the writer of the Habakkuk Commentary at Qumran does the same with the book of Habakkuk, applying the message to his own day.

We may ask whether the book of Daniel reflects the approach of the *Ḥasidim* (the pious) who were the fiercest opponents of the new anti-Jewish legislation put out by Antiochus. It does seem that the author is more at one with this group, which was ready to face death rather than contravene the Law (1 Macc. 2: 33–8), than with the Maccabees who are alluded to as those giving 'help, though small' (11: 34). It appears that the *Ḥasidim* expected that, with the re-establishment of Jewish worship in Jerusalem, the eschatological event would also occur, which would bring history, as previously understood, to an end and usher in the kingdom of God. The writer of Daniel seems to fit in with this hope (cp. 7: 25; 8: 14; 9: 27; 12: 7, 11–13).

✳ ✳ ✳ ✳ ✳ ✳ ✳ ✳ ✳ ✳ ✳ ✳ ✳

Jews at the court of Nebuchadnezzar

THE CHALLENGE TO JEWISH FAITH

1 IN THE THIRD YEAR of the reign of Jehoiakim king
of Judah, Nebuchadnezzar king of Babylon came to
2 Jerusalem and laid siege to it. The Lord delivered Jehoiakim king of Judah into his power, together with all that
was left of the vessels of the house of God; and he carried
them off to the land of Shinar, to the temple of his god,
3 where he deposited the vessels in the treasury. Then the
king ordered Ashpenaz, his chief eunuch, to take certain
of the Israelites exiles, of the blood royal and of the
4 nobility, who were to be young men of good looks and
bodily without fault, at home in all branches of knowledge, well-informed, intelligent, and fit for service in
the royal court; and he was to instruct them in the
5 literature and language of the Chaldaeans. The king
assigned them a daily allowance of food and wine from
the royal table. Their training was to last for three years,
and at the end of that time they would*ª* enter the royal
service.
6   Among them there were certain young men from
7 Judah called Daniel, Hananiah, Mishael and Azariah; but
the master of the eunuchs gave them new names: Daniel
he called Belteshazzar, Hananiah Shadrach, Mishael
8 Meshach and Azariah Abed-nego. Now Daniel deter-

[a] at the end...would: *or* all of them were to.

mined not to contaminate himself by touching the food
and wine assigned to him by the king, and he begged the
master of the eunuchs not to make him do so. God made 9
the master show kindness and goodwill to Daniel, and he 10
said to him, 'I am afraid of my lord the king: he has
assigned you your food and drink, and if he sees you
looking dejected, unlike the other young men of your
own age, it will cost me my head.' Then Daniel said to 11
the guard whom the master of the eunuchs had put in
charge of Hananiah, Mishael, Azariah and himself, 'Sub- 12
mit us to this test for ten days. Give us only vegetables to
eat and water to drink; then compare our looks with those 13
of the young men who have lived on the food assigned by
the king, and be guided in your treatment of us by what you
see.'[a] The guard listened to what they said and tested 14
them for ten days. At the end of ten days they looked 15
healthier and were better nourished than all the young
men who had lived on the food assigned them by the
king. So the guard took away the assignment of food and 16
the wine they were to drink, and gave them only the
vegetables.

To all four of these young men God had given know- 17
ledge and understanding of books and learning of every
kind, while Daniel had a gift for interpreting visions and
dreams of every kind. The time came which the king had 18
fixed for introducing the young men to court, and the
master of the eunuchs brought them into the presence of
Nebuchadnezzar. The king talked with them and found 19
none of them to compare with Daniel, Hananiah, Mishael
and Azariah; so they entered the royal service. Whenever 20

[a] be guided...see: *or* treat us as you see fit.

the king consulted them on any matter calling for insight and judgement, he found them ten times better than all
21 the magicians and exorcists in his whole kingdom. Now Daniel was there till the first year of King Cyrus.

* For the writer Babylon stands for man's attempt to establish for himself an earthly paradise. In Gen. 11 the tower of Babel (= Babylon) was constructed by men who desired to storm the heights of heaven, and we know that the hanging gardens of Babylon, dating to the time of Nebuchadnezzar, were among the wonders of the ancient world. Babylon, the human edifice, is seen as opposed to Jerusalem, the city of God. Nebuchadnezzar appears, therefore, not simply as an historic figure of the past, the captor of Jerusalem in 586 B.C.; he is at the same time the type of all opponents of the divine city and the divine order. In this chapter we are introduced to Daniel and his three companions at the Babylonian court, where the challenges to Jewish faith and practice they experienced were similar to those met by Jews abroad and in Palestine itself, as a result of the hellenizing policy of the Greek kings. Were the Jews to lose their exclusive character and to become assimilated to the peoples around them, or did loyalty to the faith, as enshrined in the Jewish Law, demand that they remain separate from the Gentiles? The writer is keen to stress in this chapter the distinctive character of the Jewish people and to assert that only when they are obedient to the demands of the Law will they be blessed by God.

1. *In the third year*: according to 2 Kings 23: 36 Jehoiakim reigned for eleven years (608–597 B.C.) and there is no reference to any capture of Jerusalem in 606 B.C., as implied here. In any case, Nebuchadnezzar only became king in 604 B.C. on the death of his father (see Jer. 25: 1). The writer here follows the tradition in 2 Kings 24: 1 and 2 Chron. 36: 6–7, which refers to an attack on Jerusalem after Jehoiakim had revolted, after paying tribute to Babylon for three years.

Jehoiakim had become a vassal after Nebuchadnezzar had defeated Egypt at Carchemish, but in 601 B.C. (three years later) Nebuchadnezzar engaged in a fur·her campaign against Egypt, which proved a failure. Possibly Jehoiakim ceased to pay allegiance to Babylon from then, and the 'third year' may then be an echo of an historical situation. By dating the first capture of Jerusalem to 606 B.C. instead of 597 B.C. the writer is able to extend the exile to the seventy years foretold by Jeremiah (Jer. 25: 11–12; 29: 10). Whilst the Hebrew Old Testament gives us Nebuchadnezzar, Nebuchadrezzar is closer to the original name *Nabu-kudurri-uṣur* (= 'Nabu protect my boundary stone').

2. The title *Lord* here does not stand for YAHWEH, but is actually 'Adonai' (= 'my L d'), the title for God, which replaced the personal name in later times. Apart from Dan. 9 (where the N.E.B. distinguishes between *Lord* (= Adonai) and LORD (= YAHWEH)) it is not used elsewhere in this book. *the land of Shinar*: this is the ancient name given to the area around Babylon in the Old Testament. The tower of Babel (Gen. 11: 2) is built in the land of Shinar. *his god*: Nebuchadnezzar's god will have been Bel or Marduk, whose temple was by the banks of the Euphrates in Babylon.

3. The word used for *nobility* is a Persian loan-word, only found elsewhere in the Old Testament in Esther 1: 3 (N.E.B. 'nobles') and 6: 9 (N.E.B. 'most honourable').

4. Whereas the name *Chaldaean* is normally used in an ethnic sense of the inhabitants of Southern Mesopotamia, the book of Daniel reflects later Graeco-Roman usage, which saw in the Chaldaeans a professional class of astrologers, magicians and wise men.

5. The Greek writer, Xenophon, refers to the custom of providing food from the table of the Persian king for favoured attendants, and 2 Kings 25: 28–30 refers to similar treatment of Jehoiachin in his exile. The word for an *allowance* of food and wine is a Persian loan-word and occurs again several times in this chapter and also in 11: 26.

19

6f. The four youths are given new names which are no longer compounded with -el (= God) or -iah (= YAHWEH the God of Israel), but with Babylonian deities. It became common for Jews in foreign service to have foreign names. In times immediately after the exile we have prominent Jews such as Zerubbabel and Sheshbazzar. Daniel is called *Belteshazzar* (meaning 'protect the life of the king'), of which name the *Bel* is understood as echoing the name of the Babylonian god (see 4: 8). The other names *Shadrach*, *Meshach* and *Abed-nego* distort the names of Babylonian deities (with the first two possibly concealing the name 'Marduk' in mangled form and the last obviously standing for the 'servant of Nebo' (or Nabu)). Apart from the mangling, no exception is taken to the use of the foreign names, and they are duly accepted as alternative names (cp. 4: 19). This practice was very common in the Greek period and encouraged in the hellenizing policy of the Ptolemies and Seleucids. For example, 2 Macc. 4: 7 refers to the brother of Onias, the High Priest, as Jason (his name being changed from Jesus).

8. Daniel had been prepared to serve in the foreign court and accept a foreign name, but he would not break Jewish tradition by unquestioningly eating any kind of food set before him. There were three reasons for rejecting the food and drink offered him:

(i)   It might belong to foods strictly taboo under the law (see Lev. 11: 2–47);

(ii) it might not be free of blood (see Deut. 12: 23–4);

(iii) it might be meat offered to idols and so involve the eater in the pagan ritual.

See 1 Macc. 1: 62–3 for a reference to those who, in their loyalty to the dietary laws of Judaism, were even prepared to die rather than eat the food which was pressed upon them by the Greeks (cp. also 2 Macc. 5: 27; 6: 18–31). The force of tradition is very strong and dietary laws still prevent full table fellowship between Jews and Gentiles. It is important to say that mere expediency or compromise are insufficient reasons for setting aside age-long customs. As Mark 7: 19 and Acts 10: 9–16 indicate, they are only set aside in the light of principles seen to be even more fundamental. *the master of the eunuchs*: it is unlikely that he actually was a eunuch. The term seems to indicate a royal official. In the story of Joseph, Potiphar is also described as a 'eunuch' (Gen. 39: 1), but he was a married man (see Gen. 39: 7–20). The fact that some officials actually were eunuchs led to the term 'eunuch' being used as an equivalent for 'official'. An important 'official' was in charge of the king's *harem* (his wives), and he was undoubtedly a eunuch. This may have been the reason for the confusion in the meaning of the term.

9. The emphasis here is that God had not abdicated his authority; he is still in control (1: 15–16). As a result, the four youths are allowed to follow their own strict diet and verses 10–15 show the blessings that followed a faithful adherence to the demands of the Law.

17. From this verse the story turns from the whole question of diet to an emphasis upon the wisdom and accomplishments of the four and the consequent high regard with which they were held. There is a very obvious echo of the Joseph stories, for Joseph, too, when far from home, impresses first Potiphar, then the prison officer and, finally, Pharaoh himself with his wisdom and discretion. As in the case of Joseph (see Gen. 41: 37–9), so here God is seen as the source of *knowledge and understanding*. He alone can give the 'interpretation' (an important word in Daniel and in subsequent apocalyptic writings) of *visions and dreams*. Notice how Daniel and his friends outdo the native experts at their own game! As God is the one who bestows wisdom, the wisdom he grants must far outshine the wisdom of the Babylonian magicians.

20. *he found them ten times better*: the benefit accruing to Nebuchadnezzar is seen as a by-product of the faithfulness of the four youths to their God.

21. *the first year of King Cyrus*: this verse speaks of Daniel as

still alive when Cyrus came to the throne (presumably the throne of Babylon). There is no necessary contradiction with 10: 1 which refers to the 'third year' of Cyrus. The Hebrew of 1: 21 seems to be defective and it is possible that the original text had 'Daniel remained in royal service till Cyrus became king'. As the author thinks of Daniel serving Darius 'the Mede' after the capture of Babylon (see 6: 2) and considers Cyrus to have succeeded Darius, he might have thought Daniel too old to serve under Cyrus, but still able to receive visions even in the third year of Cyrus' reign. ✻

NEBUCHADNEZZAR'S DREAM

2 In the second year of his reign Nebuchadnezzar had dreams, and his mind was so troubled that he could not
2 sleep. Then the king gave orders to summon the magicians, exorcists, sorcerers, and Chaldaeans to tell him what he had dreamt. They came in and stood in the royal
3 presence, and the king said to them, 'I have had a dream and my mind has been troubled to know what my dream
4 was.' The Chaldaeans, speaking in Aramaic, said,*a* 'Long live the king ! Tell us what you dreamt and we will tell
5 you the interpretation.' The king answered, 'This is my declared intention. If you do not tell me both dream and interpretation, you shall be torn in pieces and your
6 houses shall be forfeit.*b* But if you can tell me the dream and the interpretation, you will be richly rewarded and loaded with honours. Tell me, therefore, the dream and
7 its interpretation.' They answered a second time, 'Let the king tell his servants the dream, and we will tell him the
8 interpretation.' The king answered, 'It is clear to me that

[a] *The Aramaic text begins here and continues to the end of ch. 7.*
[b] *Or* made into a dunghill (*mng. of Aram. word uncertain*).

you are trying to gain time, because you see that my intention has been declared. If you do not make known 9 to me the dream, there is one law that applies to you, and one only. What is more, you have agreed among yourselves to tell me a pack of lies to my face in the hope that with time things may alter. Tell me the dream, therefore, and I shall know that you can give me the interpretation.' The Chaldaeans answered in the presence of the king, 10 'Nobody on earth can tell your majesty what you wish to know; no great king or prince has ever made such a demand of magician, exorcist, or Chaldaean. What your 11 majesty requires of us is too hard; there is no one but the gods, who dwell remote from mortal men, who can give you the answer.' At this the king lost his temper and in a 12 great rage ordered the death of all the wise men of Babylon. A decree was issued that the wise men were to 13 be executed, and accordingly men were sent to fetch Daniel and his companions for execution.

When Arioch, the captain of the king's bodyguard, 14 was setting out to execute the wise men of Babylon, Daniel approached him cautiously and with discretion and said, 'Sir, you represent the king; why has his 15 majesty issued such a peremptory decree?' Arioch explained everything; so Daniel went in to the king's presence 16 and begged for a certain time by which he would give the king the interpretation. Then Daniel went home and 17 told the whole story to his companions, Hananiah, Mishael and Azariah. They should ask the God of heaven 18 in his mercy, he said, to disclose this secret, so that they and he with the rest of the wise men of Babylon should not be put to death. Then in a vision by night the secret 19

was revealed to Daniel, and he blessed the God of heaven
20 in these words:

> Blessed be God's name from age to age,
>   for all wisdom and power are his.
21 He changes seasons and times;
>   he deposes kings and sets them up;
>   he gives wisdom to the wise
>   and all their store of knowledge to the men who
>   know;
22 he reveals deep mysteries;
>   he knows what lies in darkness,
>   and light has its dwellings with him.
23 To thee, God of my fathers, I give thanks
>   and praise,
>   for thou hast given me wisdom and power;
>   thou hast now revealed to me what we asked,
>   and told us what the king is concerned to know.

24   Daniel therefore[a] went to Arioch who had been charged
by the king to put to death the wise men of Babylon and
said to him, 'Do not put the wise men of Babylon to
death. Take me into the king's presence, and I will now
25 tell him the interpretation of the dream.' Arioch in great
trepidation brought Daniel before the king and said to
him, 'I have found among the Jewish exiles a man who
will make known to your majesty the interpretation of
26 your dream.' Thereupon the king said to Daniel (who
was also called Belteshazzar), 'Can you tell me what I
27 saw in my dream and interpret it?' Daniel answered in
the king's presence, 'The secret about which your

[a] *So Sept.; Aram. adds* went in.

majesty inquires no wise man, exorcist, magician, or diviner can disclose to you. But there is in heaven a god 28 who reveals secrets, and he has told King Nebuchadnezzar what is to be at the end of this age. This is the dream and these the visions that came into your head: the thoughts 29 that came to you, O king, as you lay on your bed, were thoughts of things to come, and the revealer of secrets has made known to you what is to be. This secret has 30 been revealed to me not because I am wise beyond all living men, but because your majesty is to know the interpretation and understand the thoughts which have entered your mind.'

* There is a close parallel in this chapter with the story of Joseph and his ability to interpret dreams (see Gen. 41). Daniel, like Joseph, is the recipient of a divine gift. The author brings out the strong contrast between the attitude of the Babylonian king and that of Daniel. On the one side we have fear (verse 3), leading to threatening (verse 5) and violence (verse 12), but all to no avail; on the other we have Daniel's faith (verses 14–24), marked by prayer (verse 18) and a spirit of thanksgiving (verses 20–3). God is not bound by fate; he is the Lord of history, who 'gives wisdom' (verse 21). 'Light has its dwelling with him' (verse 22) and so he is able to penetrate through the darkness, solving problems and mysteries. Daniel's thanksgiving refers to the personal dealings of God with man – 'thou hast now revealed to *me* what we asked, and told *us* what the king is concerned to know' (verse 23). Faith is seen, therefore, as based

    (1) on the being of God (verse 20);

    (2) on his sovereignty, which means that nothing is beyond his control (verse 21);

    (3) on the personal concern of God (verse 23).

Like much of the later wisdom literature, the story emphasizes the transcendent character of wisdom; only a divine disclosure can make it available to man. The book of Job asserts that 'God understands the way to it, he alone knows its source' (Job 28: 23). Daniel, too, is conscious of this, and that fact is the basis both of his humility (verse 27) and his boldness (verse 30).

1. *In the second year of his reign*: there must be a mistake in calling this 'the second year' of Nebuchadnezzar's reign. In 1: 5 Daniel is said to begin a period of three years' training, and in 1: 18 there is reference to the completion of the course, whilst 2: 48 refers to him as made a ruler over a province. If the chronology of this verse were correct, Daniel would be a ruler before his graduation! Some have argued that the writer knowing from Jer. 46: 2 of the great victory of Carchemish, dating to the fourth year of Jehoiakim's reign, has reckoned the third year of Jehoiakim (see ch. 1: 1) as the first year of Nebuchadnezzar and so the second year of his reign would have been the year of his greatest triumph. This chapter is saying that this was the year when he was to discover that God is greater than any earthly ruler. *Nebuchadnezzar had dreams*: it seems to have been common for rulers to believe that there was a special significance in their dreams. The Philistine king Abimelech receives the divine warning in a dream (Gen. 20: 3), a dream reveals the future to Pharaoh (Gen. 41: 1) and King Solomon has his dream (1 Kings 3: 5–14).

2. At Babylon the court seers had the responsibility of interpreting the king's dreams, and he calls for his *magicians, exorcists, sorcerers, and Chaldaeans*. Note how the writer loves to enumerate lists of different functions or objects (cp. 3: 2–3, 4–5, 21). The sorcerers would normally be responsible for muttering charms or ritual incantations. The Chaldaeans were the special group of 'wise men'. The enumeration indicates that every conceivable man of wisdom is called to the king's assistance.

4. *speaking in Aramaic*: with the reference to the Chaldaeans' speech the language of the text changes from Hebrew to Aramaic and the Aramaic continues until the end of ch. 7. The Babylonian 'wise men' would not have spoken in Aramaic (the language commonly used throughout the Fertile Crescent), but Babylonian or Assyrian. *interpretation*: the word used comes from a root meaning 'unloose' and so conveys the idea of 'releasing a hidden meaning'. In many writings of the Qumran community, discovered near the Dead Sea, the word is used of the special interpretation of biblical passages.

5. Nebuchadnezzar demands both the dream and the interpretation not necessarily because he has forgotten the dream, but because he is sceptical of the true ability of the 'wise men' to do any more than apply set formulae and wants a guarantee of their inspiration. The threatening indicates the king's frustration. *torn in pieces*: the word translated *in pieces* (also used in 3: 29) literally means a 'member' or 'limb' and is Iranian in origin.

10. *Nobody on earth can tell...what you wish to know*: here we have the most telling statement about human impotence. What man cannot do God can achieve.

13. *men were sent to fetch Daniel and his companions*: it appears that Daniel knew nothing about the dream until the guards set out to kill him and his friends as members of the order of Chaldaeans. It is asserted at 1: 20 that the king had already found them to be the best of his wise men, and yet they were not among the group first summoned to the king in ch. 2. This is probably an indication that we have in these early chapters what were originally a string of separate stories.

14f. The *peremptory* character of the decree is seen in the fact that possible interpreters have not yet been consulted. Daniel, therefore, asks for more time, in order that he may save the reputation of his caste. He recognizes, however, that the disclosure of the secret (verse 18) is only possible through the mercy of God.

18. *God of heaven*: this is the Jewish equivalent of the Canaanite god, *Ba'al Shāmēm*, and was used by the Persians for the God of the Jews. It later fell out of use because it resembled too much the Greek title *Zeus Ouranios*. The title occurs four times in this chapter. *disclose this secret*: the old Persian word *raz* is used. It occurs many times in this chapter and elsewhere only in 4: 9.

19. *in a vision by night*: there seems to be emphasis on the vision as being more significant than a dream. There is a possible link with Jacob's vision (Gen. 46: 2), when he was assured of God's presence with him on his journey to Egypt. The prophets are sometimes described as receiving their visions *by night* (cp. Zech. 1: 8).

21–3. The prayer of thanksgiving rejects the idea of the influence of the stars on human fate and history. Instead we have emphasis on God's omnipotence and universal control. There is also emphasis on his revelation (cp. Job 12: 12 and 13). For the disclosure of the *mysteries*, cp. 'He uncovers mysteries deep in obscurity and into thick darkness he brings light '(Job 12: 22).

25. *I have found…a man*: the language seems to suggest that this was Daniel's first audience with the king, although 1: 19 suggests that he was well known to the king and 2: 16 speaks of a previous audience to secure a stay in the order of execution. We can only suppose that the author was not concerned to mould his sources into a consistent whole. He desires rather to say that it is the God of the Jews (for Daniel is *among the Jewish exiles*) who both governs all things and reveals his intentions (see 2: 28).

28. *the end of this age*: this phrase occurs fourteen times in the Old Testament and its meaning depends on the situation in which the writer is living. It nearly always indicates a time of crisis in Israelite history (cp. Gen. 49: 1; Num. 24: 14: in both cases translated 'days to come' in the N.E.B.), but then points to the end of the present age and the inauguration of the new age of God's rule (cp. Isa. 2: 2; Jer. 23: 20). ✳

THE EARTHLY EMPIRES AND THE
DIVINE KINGDOM

'As you watched, O king, you saw a great image. This 31
image, huge and dazzling, towered before you, fearful
to behold. The head of the image was of fine gold, its 32
breast and arms of silver, its belly and thighs of bronze,*a*
its legs of iron, its feet part iron and part clay. While you 33, 34
looked, a stone was hewn from a mountain,*b* not by
human hands; it struck the image on its feet of iron and
clay and shattered them. Then the iron, the clay, the bronze, 35
the silver, and the gold, were all shattered to fragments
and were swept away like chaff before the wind from a
threshing-floor in summer, until no trace of them remained. But the stone which struck the image grew into
a great mountain filling the whole earth. That was the 36
dream. We shall now tell your majesty the interpretation.
You, O king, king of kings, to whom the God of heaven 37
has given the kingdom with all its power, authority, and
honour; in whose hands he has placed men and beasts 38
and birds of the air, wherever they dwell, granting you
sovereignty over them all – you are that head of gold.
After you there shall arise another kingdom, inferior to 39
yours, and yet a third kingdom, of bronze, which shall
have sovereignty over the whole world. And there shall 40
be a fourth kingdom, strong as iron; as iron shatters and
destroys all things, it shall break and shatter the whole
earth.*c* As, in your vision, the feet and toes were part 41
potter's clay and part iron, it shall be a divided kingdom.

[*a*] Or copper.   [*b*] from a mountain: *so Sept.; Aram. om.*
[*c*] the whole earth: *prob. rdg.; Aram.* and like iron which shatters all
these.

Its core shall be partly of iron just as you saw iron mixed
42 with the common clay; as the toes were part iron and part
clay, the kingdom shall be partly strong and partly brittle.
43 As, in your vision, the iron was mixed with common
clay, so shall men mix with each other by intermarriage,
but such alliances shall not be stable: iron does not mix
44 with clay. In the period of those kings the God of heaven
will establish a kingdom which shall never be destroyed;
that kingdom shall never pass to another people; it shall
shatter and make an end of all these kingdoms, while it
45 shall itself endure for ever. This is the meaning of your
vision of the stone being hewn from a mountain, not by
human hands, and then shattering the iron, the bronze,
the clay, the silver, and the gold. The mighty God has
made known to your majesty what is to be hereafter.
The dream is sure and the interpretation to be trusted.'

✶ The dream of Nebuchadnezzar is depicted as dealing with
a succession of empires through the symbolism of an image
which embraces a number of different metals. The golden
head stands for Babylon, the silver for the Medes, the bronze
for Persia and the iron for Greece, whilst the mingling of
iron and clay in the feet stands for the division of Alexander's
empire. The choice of metals suggests a gradual decline, but
that is not emphaiszed in the interpretation of the dream. We
are concerned not necessarily with succeeding epochs, but
with a succession of imperial powers. Nor is it clear that they
came after one another in historical succession. The fact that
the stone destroys them all (verses 33–4) may point to the
empires as almost co-existing. What is important for the
writer is the eternal kingdom of God which is to replace all
human principalities and powers. The empires may have

embraced only a few centuries of human history, but, in another sense, they represent the entirety of human history. The stone which destroys all is the symbol of God's judgement which is decisive and final. This is the only place in the Old Testament where human history is described in terms of ages, symbolized by metals. Some see Iranian influence, for a writing from the ninth century A.D. (containing ancient material) speaks of four periods of 1000 years (each symbolized by a metal), following the birth of Zoroaster. Others would emphasize Greek influence, as the Greek poet Hesiod, writing in the eighth century B.C., used the same four metals as Daniel (gold, silver, bronze and iron) to describe the ages of world history. Daniel appears to take over some such material, although he rejects the Greek cyclical view of history, which sees a constant repetition of the path from splendour to decline. Nebuchadnezzar is specifically linked with the first kingdom (2: 37–8; cp. Jer. 27: 6–8) and the next two empires must be Media and Persia (see Dan. 5: 28; 8: 20), even though Daniel does not postulate a total separation of the two. The Roman general Scipio, at the destruction of Carthage in 146 B.C., spoke of Rome as successor to four great world empires, the four being Assyria, Media, Persia and Macedonia. This would be more historically correct, but the writer of Daniel sees the dream as concerned with the future (2: 29, 45) and so Assyria would have no relevance. The story must begin in the present and then move into the future. Hence, Babylonia replaces Assyria as the first empire, for the reign of Nebuchadnezzar provides the dramatic starting-point. If 'four' is understood as the ultimate number, then the expectation of the final consummation of history becomes understandable.

31. *you saw a great image*: it has been suggested that the imagery is based upon the huge statues of Babylonian art, such as the statue of Bel at Babylon, described by the Greek historian Herodotus (Book I. 183). There is no suggestion, however, in the story that the image is an idol; it is parallel

rather with huge symbolical figures in human form, where the human figure represents the world.

33. *part iron and part clay*: some suggest that there was a core of clay, covered with metal (cp. Daniel, Bel, and the Snake 7).

34. *not by human hands*: there is emphasis on the divine action. Similarly, Antiochus meets his fate 'not by human hands' (8: 25). The blow is seen to strike the feet, weak because of their composite character, but it destroys the total image. (Cp. Isa. 41: 15-16; Jer. 51: 20-3; Mic. 4: 13 for the common prophetic imagery of God's judgement.)

35. *filling the whole earth*: the expansion of the stone is the symbol of the universality of God's kingdom. Perhaps we can see the influence of Ezekiel who used a mountain to symbolize the coming messianic kingdom (see Ezek. 17: 22-4).

37f. The authority of Nebuchadnezzar is seen as incorporating nature as well as the world of men. The influence of Jeremiah is evident (cp. Jer. 27: 6-7; 28: 14), where the king exercises the royal power given to man in the creation narrative (Gen. 1: 26). Some commentators see the background to these verses in the Babylonian New Year festival, when the king represented the god Marduk in the dramatic representation of the epic of creation, in which Marduk demonstrated his royal authority over the whole world. *king of kings*: this title was used of Persian kings (cp. Ezra 7: 12), but was probably not used in Babylon.

39. Media and Persia, the kingdoms of silver and bronze, are dismissed in a verse, because interest concentrates on the fourth kingdom.

40. The kingdom, *strong as iron*, is obviously that of Alexander the Great, but the division of his empire is indicated in the following verse. *the whole earth*: the N.E.B. emends the text, but if 'all these' (the footnote reading) is correct, one can only suppose that the writer sees fragments of the earlier empires still surviving to be crushed by Alexander.

42. *partly strong and partly brittle*: it is possible that the Seleucids are seen as the 'strong' and the Ptolemies in Egypt as the 'brittle'. Certainly, by the time of Antiochus III, the superiority of the northern kingdom was established, and Palestine came under Seleucid control.

43. This verse seems to presuppose the marriage between members of the Seleucid and Ptolemaic dynasties, which are mentioned more explicitly in 11: 6, 17.

44. *God...will establish a kingdom*: we move here from history to the climactic end of history, the point of divine salvation (cp. 7: 27; 9: 24; 12: 1-3).

45. *The dream is sure and the interpretation to be trusted*: great emphasis is laid on the absolute certainty of the prediction. Cp. 8: 26, where the interpretation is seen as remaining hidden till the time of fulfilment. *

THE CONVERSION OF NEBUCHADNEZZAR

Then King Nebuchadnezzar prostrated himself and 46 worshipped Daniel, and gave orders that sacrifices and soothing offerings should be made to him. 'Truly,' he 47 said, 'your god is indeed God of gods and Lord over kings, a revealer of secrets, since you have been able to reveal this secret.' Then the king promoted Daniel, 48 bestowed on him many rich gifts, and made him regent over the whole province of Babylon and chief prefect over all the wise men of Babylon. Moreover at Daniel's 49 request the king put Shadrach, Meshach and Abed-nego in charge of the administration of the province of Babylon. Daniel himself, however, remained at court.

* The Greek period also saw the beginning of proselytism – with Gentiles confessing the truth of the Jewish religion and becoming adherents of the Jewish synagogues. So here

Nebuchadnezzar is represented as confessing that the God of the Jews is the 'God of gods and Lord over kings' (verse 47). In the story of Naaman (2 Kings 5: 15-19) we have an illustration of a conversion to the faith of Israel (see especially 2 Kings 5: 17). The theme of 'conversion' is repeated in Daniel in the story of the furnace (3: 28-9), in Nebuchadnezzar's recovery from bestiality (4: 34-6) and in the story of the lions' pit (6: 26-7).

46f. *Nebuchadnezzar prostrated himself and worshipped Daniel*: the language used suggests that Daniel is himself regarded as a divine being, for the words used here are used elsewhere either of the worship of an idol (cp. 3: 5, 6, 7, 10, 15) or of man in the presence of God (cp. Gen. 17: 3; Ezek. 3: 23) or in the presence of angelic being (cp. Dan. 8: 17). The Jewish historian, Josephus, was troubled by the language and tried to interpret Nebuchadnezzar's action as his recognition of Daniel's God-given wisdom. Hence, the king venerates not so much Daniel as God who had revealed the secret to Daniel. He makes Alexander say to the high priest Jehoiada, as he venerates him, that his prostration is really to God, whose high priest Jehoiada is (*Antiquities of the Jews*, XI. 331-5). Similarly Luke indicates the reluctance of Paul to receive apparently divine honours (cp. Acts 14: 8-18; 28: 6). It is likely that Nebuchadnezzar's act reflects normal hellenistic practice in showing thanks for benefits received. Verse 47 clearly indicates that the wisdom comes from God.

48f. The story is rounded off by saying that even pagan kings may reward God's faithful servants for their faithfulness. *regent over the whole province of Babylon*: we have evidence of prefects governing different sections of the Babylonian Empire. In Persian times the province included the whole of Mesopotamia. *chief prefect over all the wise men of Babylon*: the writer is concerned to stress the elevated position gained by Daniel and accordingly sees him as leader of the Babylonian magicians. Similarly, Moses is described as 'trained in all the wisdom of the Egyptians' (Acts 7: 22). ✶

THE BLAZING FURNACE AND THE
WITNESS OF FAITH

King Nebuchadnezzar made an image of gold, ninety **3**
feet high and nine feet broad.*ª* He had it set up in the plain
of Dura in the province of Babylon. Then he sent out a **2**
summons to assemble the satraps, prefects, viceroys,
counsellors, treasurers, judges, chief constables, and all
governors of provinces to attend the dedication of the
image which he had set up. So they assembled – the **3**
satraps, prefects, viceroys, counsellors, treasurers, judges,
chief constables, and all governors of provinces – for the
dedication of the image which King Nebuchadnezzar
had set up; and they stood before the image which
Nebuchadnezzar had set up. Then the herald loudly **4**
proclaimed, 'O peoples and nations of every language,
you are commanded, when you hear the sound of horn, **5**
pipe, zither, triangle, dulcimer, music, and singing of
every kind, to prostrate yourselves and worship the golden
image which King Nebuchadnezzar has set up. Whoever **6**
does not prostrate himself and worship shall forthwith be
thrown into a blazing furnace.' Accordingly, no sooner **7**
did all the peoples hear the sound of horn, pipe, zither,
triangle, dulcimer, music,*ᵇ* and singing of every kind,
than all the peoples and nations of every language
prostrated themselves and worshipped the golden image
which King Nebuchadnezzar had set up.

It was then that certain Chaldaeans came forward and **8**
brought a charge against the Jews. They said to King **9**

[a] *Lit.* sixty cubits high and six cubits broad.
[b] music: *so many MSS.; others om.*

10 Nebuchadnezzar, 'Long live the king! Your majesty has issued an order that every man who hears the sound of horn, pipe, zither, triangle, dulcimer, music, and singing of every kind shall fall down and worship the image of
11 gold. Whoever does not do so shall be thrown into a
12 blazing furnace. There are certain Jews, Shadrach, Meshach and Abed-nego, whom you have put in charge of the administration of the province of Babylon. These men, your majesty, have taken no notice of your command; they do not serve your god, nor do they worship the
13 golden image which you have set up.' Then in rage and fury Nebuchadnezzar ordered Shadrach, Meshach and Abed-nego to be fetched, and they were brought into
14 the king's presence. Nebuchadnezzar said to them, 'Is it true, Shadrach, Meshach and Abed-nego, that you do not serve my god or worship the golden image which I
15 have set up? If you are ready at once to prostrate yourselves when you hear the sound of horn, pipe, zither, triangle, dulcimer, music, and singing of every kind, and to worship the image that I have set up, well and good. But if you do not worship it, you shall forthwith be thrown into the blazing furnace; and what god is there
16 that can save you from my power?' Shadrach, Meshach and Abed-nego said to King Nebuchadnezzar, 'We have
17 no need to answer you on this matter. If there is a god who is able to save us from the blazing furnace, it is our God whom we serve, and he will save us from your
18 power, O king; but if not, be it known to your majesty that we will neither serve your god nor worship the golden image that you have set up.'
19   Then Nebuchadnezzar flew into a rage with Shadrach,

Meshach and Abed-nego, and his face was distorted with anger. He gave orders that the furnace should be heated up to seven times its usual heat, and commanded some of 20 the strongest men in his army to bind Shadrach, Meshach and Abed-nego and throw them into the blazing furnace. Then those men in their trousers, their shirts, and their 21 hats and all their other clothes, were bound and thrown into the blazing furnace. Because the king's order was 22 urgent and the furnace exceedingly hot, the men who were carrying Shadrach, Meshach and Abed-nego were killed by the flames that leapt out; and those three men, 23 Shadrach, Meshach and Abed-nego, fell bound into the blazing furnace.

Then King Nebuchadnezzar was amazed and sprang 24 to his feet in great trepidation. He said to his courtiers, 'Was it not three men whom we threw bound into the fire?' They answered the king, 'Assuredly, your majesty.' He answered, 'Yet I see four men walking about in the 25 fire free and unharmed; and the fourth looks like a god.'[a] Nebuchadnezzar approached the door of the blazing 26 furnace and said to the men, 'Shadrach, Meshach and Abed-nego, servants of the Most High God, come out, come here.' Then Shadrach, Meshach and Abed-nego came out from the fire. And the satraps, prefects, vice- 27 roys, and the king's courtiers gathered round and saw how the fire had had no power to harm the bodies of these men; the hair of their heads had not been singed, their trousers were untouched, and no smell of fire lingered about them.

[a] *Lit.* like a son of a god.

37

✶ The object of this chapter is to encourage the Jews to maintain a steadfast loyalty to their own faith and to reject all the trappings of heathen worship. They are to welcome death rather than turn aside from the faith (see verses 17–18). The story of the fiery furnace introduces us to the persistence and utter faithfulness of Shadrach, Meshach and Abed-nego who refuse to fall in with the religious policy of Nebuchadnezzar. For a reader in the Greek period – and more particularly for one living in the time of Antiochus Epiphanes – the message would have been clear. The royal tyrant is seen as vaunting himself and apparently able to do whatever he wants. He can build (verse 1), organize parades (verse 3) and demand a complete and abject dependence on the part of his subjects (verse 5). He can show his fury (verse 13) and demonstrate a complete loss of self-control (verse 19), but he is still unable to force the faithful Jews to give up their faith. They are cast bound into the blazing furnace (verse 23), but all that the fire can do is to loose the very bonds that bound them (verse 25). What is more they found themselves in the company of another, who 'looks like a god' (verse 25). Whilst the story includes the account of a miraculous delivery, it is quite clear that the faithful Jew is encouraged to continue his witness to his faith right up to the point of death. Even the dying martyr can rest in the hope of a resurrection (see Dan. 12: 2; 2 Macc. 7).

It is likely that the story of the image and the furnace rest upon tradition. The link with Nebuchadnezzar is probably the result of the reference in Jeremiah to the men 'whom the king of Babylon roasted in the fire' (Jer. 29: 22). Isaiah 43: 2 refers not only to walking 'through fire', but also speaks of the presence of God with his people, when they suffer persecution. Psalm 66: 10–12 also speaks in general terms of God's help in times of distress, and makes particular reference to danger from 'fire and water'. Death by fire was also a penalty inflicted in Persia, and Antiochus Epiphanes used the same form of punishment in his attempt to suppress Judaism (cp. 2 Macc. 7: 4–5). It has been suggested that the tradition reflects a persecution under Nabonidus, the last Babylonian king. We have possibly hints of this in Habakkuk (cp. Hab. 1: 2) and in Second Isaiah (chs. 40–55), where the prophet speaks the word of comfort in the expectation that the victory of Cyrus over Babylon will bring to an end the long suffering of the exiles (cp. Isa. 45: 1–4).

The fact that Daniel does not feature in this chapter suggests that the story comes from an independent source. It is even possible that Shadrach, Meshach and Abed-nego were brought into an older story to link it with the other stories in this earlier section of Daniel. From the standpoint of the author of the book, the fact that he also has a story of deliverance linked with Daniel (in ch. 6) would have dispensed with the need to associate him with this story.

1. *King Nebuchadnezzar made an image*: whilst the Aramaic text does not date this story, the Greek translation gives as the date 'the eighteenth year of Nebuchadnezzar'. This would have been 586 B.C., the year of the capture of Jerusalem and the destruction of the temple. The 'eighteenth year' appears in Jer. 52: 29, while 2 Kings 25: 8 has the 'nineteenth year', a difference which may reflect different calendar systems. The dating makes the point that Nebuchadnezzar is substituting his god for the God of Israel. He destroys the temple in Jerusalem and sets up his image which not only honoured his god, but also celebrates his victory over Jerusalem. Jeremiah, like Isaiah, refers to plating 'with silver and gold' (cp. Jer. 10: 3–4). Enormous images were not unusual in the East, and the Greek historian Herodotus refers to one in the temple of Bel in Babylon (Book 1. 183). Such images were objects of mockery for Isaiah, as he speaks of the 'Holy One' as the only God (cp. Isa. 40: 19). *the plain of Dura*: scholars are uncertain of the locality of Dura. As a piece of local colour, the reference may indicate a traditional element in the story.

2. The dignitaries who are summoned to worship the

image are named in their order of precedence, and most of the titles are of Persian origin. The long list, like the repetition in verse 3, is used to build up the scene. It is as if one said 'Everyone important was there.' They were present for the dedication of the image, presumably a representation of the Babylonian god Marduk. As the king was regarded as the representative of the god, readers in the time of Antiochus Epiphanes would have seen the reference to Antiochus' claim to be a manifestation of Zeus. The worship of the image would almost involve for the Jews the worship of the king. King or Emperor worship was later to be one of the chief reasons why Christians were persecuted for their faith. Like the Jewish witnesses in this story, Christians refused to bow down before the imperial image.

4. *O peoples and nations of every language*: the different races and nationalities were represented by the officials, but the exaggerated language also indicates the king's desire to make his religion and the worship associated with it universal and a focal point of the empire's unity.

5. Of the instruments listed, two (the *horn* and the *pipe*) are of Semitic origin, whilst three (translated as *triangle*, *dulcimer* and *music* in N.E.B.) are Greek. It is thought that the *zither* was probably Semitic, but it may have been Greek. In translating the last word (*sumphonyah*) by *music* the N.E.B. is following the original meaning of a 'concord of sound', but the historian Polybius (204–122 B.C.) uses it of an instrument rather like a bagpipe, possibly a goat-skin with reed pipes. He says that it was a great favourite with Antiochus Epiphanes, and that he scandalized onlookers by dancing to it. (In verse 7, where the instruments are listed again, this one is omitted.) The horn is the equivalent of the Hebrew *shophar* (a ram's horn), sometimes translated 'trumpet' in the Old Testament. The name for the pipe is associated with a 'hissing' or 'whistling' sound. The zither is a harp-like instrument; the triangle was a small triangular instrument and had four strings. The dulcimer was also a triangular stringed instrument with a

sounding board above the strings. Some commentators have suggested that the use of all these instruments is meant to appear as a parody of the Jewish celebration at New Year, when the ram's horn was blown. For a Jew to participate in such a parody would be like a contemporary Christian participating in a black mass or a witches' sabbath.

6. The penalty for refusing to worship the image was death in the blazing kiln. It is likely that the kiln was fed from the top, and that there was an opening at the side of the bottom. When stoked up the flames would shoot up and so threaten anyone near the top (see verse 22). As the flames died down it would be possible to see (from the side) the inside of the kiln (see verses 24–5).

8–12. *certain Chaldaeans came forward and brought a charge*: the professional 'wise men' were undoubtedly jealous of the position enjoyed by the Jews (cp. 2: 49; 6: 4 and the hatred of Haman for Mordecai in the book of Esther). The phrase *brought a charge* literally means 'ate pieces of' and the words convey the idea of slander or false accusation. The Chaldaeans wished to indicate the disloyalty of the Jews who *have taken no notice of your command* (verse 12) and so gain the positions which they would forfeit, if punished.

13. *in rage and fury*: the fury of oriental rulers is a regular feature of such stories (cp. Esther 1: 12; 7: 7; Judith 5: 1; 2 Macc. 7: 3).

15. *what god...can save you from my power?*: Nebuchadnezzar is described as making the same challenge that the Assyrians made to Hezekiah in the time of the prophet Isaiah (see Isa. 36: 13–20; 37: 10–12; 2 Kings 18: 20–2, 29–35).

17f. *he will save us from your power*: the N.E.B. translation tries to make sense of a difficult text in presenting clearly the alternatives of deliverance and non-deliverance. It is strange that doubts should have been raised about deliverance in this context, but Jewish martyrs were actually put to death and not delivered. Hence, the three assert their loyalty to God, saying that they are prepared to go to their deaths for their faith rather than become apostates. There is an echo of the witness of Jeremiah who persisted in his role as a prophet despite the threats made against his life (see Jer. 26: 7–15). The three refer to *our God whom we serve* but do not use the name of God. The writing belongs to the time when reverence for the personal name of God meant that it was never spoken. At the same time there is the suggestion that Nebuchadnezzar's *god* is not divine in any way; they are only prepared to worship one who is truly God.

19f. *Nebuchadnezzar flew into a rage*: the rejection of his commands makes the king even angrier. He is not satisfied with any fire; only the hottest fire possible will satisfy him! At the same time he needs his *strongest men* to throw the Jews into the furnace, and the fact that they are fully clothed (and not stripped first) emphasizes, first, the king's demand that the punishment be immediate and, secondly, the wonder of the miracle that is to take place.

23. This verse is omitted in the Septuagint and is a weak anticlimax after the previous verses. At this point the Septuagint inserts the Song of the Three Children (see the commentary in *Shorter Books of the Apocrypha* in this series, pp. 211–23), feeling that the time in the furnace was a suitable occasion for praising God and affirming his power.

24–7. Nebuchadnezzar is startled to see *four men walking about in the fire free and unharmed*. The only effect the fire had had on the three was to destroy their bonds, but it is the presence of the fourth that causes most surprise. He is said to look *like a god*, but it is likely that the writer is thinking of an angel. The angels were thought to be attendants upon God, or members of his court, who could be sent out with messages or who could be the agents through whom the divine will was accomplished. Here the one *like a god* is undoubtedly seen as the one through whom the three had been released from their bonds. The presence of the angel symbolizes the presence of God himself with his faithful servants, as they suffer for the sake of their loyalty to his declared commands.

The king can do no more than acknowledge them to be *servants of the Most High God* and to call them out of the furnace. The title *Most High God* was originally a Canaanite one used for the supreme deity (see Gen. 14: 19–20; Num. 24: 16), but once Yahweh was seen as the supreme deity and regarded as sole ruler of all, the name *Most High God* was used by those Gentiles who had been influenced by Judaism and wished to profess their monotheistic faith. ✶

THE CONFESSION OF FAITH BY NEBUCHADNEZZAR

Then Nebuchadnezzar spoke out, 'Blessed is the God 28 of Shadrach, Meshach and Abed-nego. He has sent his angel to save his servants who put their trust in him, who disobeyed the royal command and were willing to yield themselves to the fire*a* rather than to serve or worship any god other than their own God. I therefore issue a decree 29 that any man, to whatever people or nation he belongs, whatever his language, if he speaks blasphemy against the God of Shadrach, Meshach and Abed-nego, shall be torn to pieces and his house shall be forfeit;*b* for there is no other god who can save men in this way.' Then the 30 king advanced the fortunes of Shadrach, Meshach and Abed-nego in the province of Babylon.

✶ Here, as in 2: 46–9, the king is represented as affirming his faith in the God of the Jews. He acknowledges that no other god could possibly 'save men in this way' (verse 29). Whereas the royal decree had previously demanded worship of the man-made things, now a royal decree demands a universal recognition of the unique power of 'the God of

[a] to the fire: *so Sept.; Aram. om*
[b] *Or* made into a dunghill (*mng. of Aram. word uncertain*).

Shadrach, Meshach and Abed-nego'. There is no demand that
he should be the only God worshipped. Rather the Jewish
faith is declared to be permissible within his realm. For the
Jews in the reign of Antiochus Epiphanes the story would
have been heard as an encouragement to persist faithfully as
Jews in the face of persecution. Whilst the king might not
actually be converted, at least they could win religious
tolerance for themselves.

30. The writer is often anxious to emphasize the reward
that comes from faithfulness to God. In the same way Job,
at the conclusion of his suffering, is said to have become far
more prosperous than he had ever been before (see Job 42:
10–17). ✻

NEBUCHADNEZZAR DREAMS OF JUDGEMENT

4 1*a* King Nebuchadnezzar to all peoples and nations of every
language living in the whole world: May all prosperity
2 be yours! It is my pleasure to recount the signs and
marvels which the Most High God has worked for me:

3   How great are his signs,
      and his marvels overwhelming!
      His kingdom is an everlasting kingdom,
      his sovereignty stands to all generations.

4*b* I, Nebuchadnezzar, was living peacefully at home in the
5 luxury of my palace. As I lay on my bed, I saw a dream
which terrified me; and fantasies and visions which came
6 into my head dismayed me. So I issued an order summoning into my presence all the wise men of Babylon to make
7 known to me the interpretation of the dream. Then the
magicians, exorcists, Chaldaeans, and diviners came in,

[a] *3:31 in Aram.*   [b] *4:1 in Aram.*

and in their presence I related my dream. But they could
not interpret it. And yet another came into my presence, 8
Daniel, who is called Belteshazzar after the name of my
god, a man possessed by the spirit of the holy gods. To
him, too, I related the dream: 'Belteshazzar, chief of the 9
magicians, whom I myself know to be possessed by the
spirit of the holy gods, and whom no secret baffles, listen
to[a] the vision I saw in a dream, and tell me its interpretation.

'Here is the vision which came into my head as I was 10
lying upon my bed:

> As I was looking,
> I saw a tree of great height at the centre of the earth;
>> the tree grew and became strong, 11
> reaching with its top to the sky
>> and visible to earth's farthest bounds.
>> Its foliage was lovely, 12
>> and its fruit abundant;
> and it yielded food for all.
> Beneath it the wild beasts found shelter,
> the birds lodged in its branches,
> and from it all living creatures fed.

'Here is another vision which came into my head as I 13
was lying upon my bed:

> As I was watching, there was a Watcher,
> a Holy One coming down from heaven.
> He cried aloud and said, 14
> "Hew down the tree, lop off the branches,
> strip away the foliage, scatter the fruit.

[a] listen to: *so Theod.; Aram. om.*

Let the wild beasts flee from its shelter
and the birds from its branches,
15 but leave the stump with its roots in the ground.
So, tethered with an iron ring,
let him eat his fill of the lush grass;
let him be drenched with the dew of heaven
and share the lot of the beasts in their pasture;
16 let his mind cease to be a man's mind,
and let him be given the mind of a beast.
Let seven times pass over him.
17 The issue has been determined by the Watchers
and the sentence pronounced by the Holy Ones.

Thereby the living will know that the Most High is sovereign in the kingdom of men: he gives the kingdom to whom he will and he may set over it the humblest of mankind."

18 'This is the dream which I, King Nebuchadnezzar, have dreamed; now, Belteshazzar, tell me its interpretation; for, though all the wise men of my kingdom are unable to tell me what it means, you can tell me, since the spirit of the holy gods is in you.'

19 Daniel, who was called Belteshazzar, was dumbfounded for a moment, dismayed by his thoughts; but the king said, 'Do not let the dream and its interpretation dismay you.' Belteshazzar answered, 'My lord, if only the dream were for those who hate you and its interpretation for
20 your enemies! The tree which you saw grow and become strong, reaching with its top to the sky and visible to
21 earth's farthest bounds, its foliage lovely and its fruit abundant, a tree which yielded food for all, beneath

46

which the wild beasts dwelt and in whose branches the birds lodged, that tree, O king, is you. You have grown 22 and become strong. Your power has grown and reaches the sky; your sovereignty stretches to the ends of the earth. Also, O king, you saw a Watcher, a Holy One, 23 coming down from heaven and saying, "Hew down the tree and destroy it, but leave its stump with its roots in the ground. So, tethered with an iron ring, let him eat his fill of the lush grass; let him be drenched with the dew of heaven and share the lot of the beasts until seven times pass over him." This is the interpretation, O king – it is a 24 decree of the Most High which touches my lord the king. You will be banished from the society of men; you will 25 have to live with the wild beasts; you will feed on grass like oxen and you will be drenched with the dew of heaven. Seven times will pass over you until you have learnt that the Most High is sovereign over the kingdom of men and gives it to whom he will. The command was 26 given to leave the stump of the tree with its roots. By this you may know that from the time you acknowledge the sovereignty of heaven your rule will endure. Be 27 advised by me, O king: redeem your sins by charity and your iniquities by generosity to the wretched. So may you long enjoy peace of mind.'

* In this chapter Nebuchadnezzar is represented as describing the circumstances which had led him to acclaim the truth that God's 'kingdom is an everlasting kingdom' and the enduring character of God's sovereignty (verse 3). The background to his experience was ease and luxury (verse 4), but this was no guarantee against neurotic anxiety. Human wisdom

proved unable to solve the king's problems highlighted by his dream (verse 7). By contrast with the ineffectiveness of the professional 'wise men', Daniel is presented as 'a man possessed by the spirit of the holy gods' (verse 8), a man 'whom no secret baffles' (verse 9). The dream portrays Nebuchadnezzar as the father of his people – the tree 'reaching with its top to the sky' (verse 10), but the heathen power is seen to be helpless, if it seeks to stand against God or substitute its own authority for the sovereignty of God. When the king goes beyond his human bounds, he is hurled back by the 'Watcher' (verse 13), the angelic guardian of God's honour (cp. verses 17, 25, 32, 34). The word of doom is spoken, and the king is taught that to deny God his place is to become sub-human. Up to verse 18 the story is given in the first person, as though the king were in direct communication with his people, but from verse 19 the account shifts to the third person and is narrative in form. Daniel interprets the dream in terms of God's judgement upon the king whose 'sovereignty stretches to the ends of the earth' (verse 22), but the judgement is not seen as final. There is a place for salvation and restoration; the tree may be overthrown, but a stump recovers from which new life can blossom forth (verse 26) after the seven years of judgement.

This chapter raises once again historical questions, as we have no record of Nebuchadnezzar's madness or departure from the seat of government for a period of seven years. The historian Megasthenes, writing about 300 B.C., refers to the fact that 'Nebuchadnezzar was inspired by some god or other, and spoke of a calamity from the roof of his palace' and some would see here a basis for the story. More likely, however, is the theory which links the story with Nabonidus, the last Babylonian king, who was the father of Belshazzar, the 'ruler' who features in ch. 5. Among the manuscripts found near the Dead Sea in Cave IV is a small Aramaic scroll entitled 'The Prayer of Nabonidus', in which the king speaks of being 'smitten with a malignant disease', as a result of which he became unlike men for a period of seven years. He confessed his sins and received help from a Jewish magician 'among those exiled in Babylon'. He is told to give glory 'to the Name of the Most High God', if he is to regain his health. The parallels are too close to be accidental, and it is likely, therefore, that the story in ch. 4 was originally about Nabonidus. The fact that he had gained a general reputation in Babylon for religious laxity is also significant. As we know so little about his long stay at Teima in Arabia, it is quite possible to fit in a time of mental illness into his time there. There are also close parallels in the story with the pattern of Greek tragedy, where *hubris*, the exhibition of over-weening pride, leads inexorably to *nemesis*, the divine judgement upon any who exceed the bounds of what it is to be human. Here a wilful persistence in idolatry and an attempt at self-deification leads to loss of the human image and the brutalizing of man.

We possess two forms of this chapter. The Aramaic text in the Hebrew Old Testament presents the whole narrative as a kind of imperial pronouncement given to all his subjects. The Greek translation (the Septuagint) omits the first three verses, and introduces verse 4 with the words, 'In the eighteenth year of his reign Nebuchadnezzar said...' The Septuagint also omits reference to the summoning of the wise men (verses 6–7) and immediately tells of Daniel's encounter with the king. The decree is placed at the very end of the story, making it parallel with the stories in chs. 3 and 6. It seems clear that this section of the book was preserved in variant forms.

1. The formula used at the beginning is similar to that used in ancient letters and decrees (cp. the letter in Ezra 5: 8 and the proclamation of Cyrus as recorded in Ezra 1: 2f.; it also occurs in Aramaic papyri from Elephantine in Egypt and elsewhere). *living in the whole world*: these words are an obvious exaggeration, but indicate the somewhat grandiose claims of the king.

2f. The doxology anticipates the truth to be taught by

the chapter as a whole, and especially the language of verse
34. There are echoes of Ps. 145: 13. *signs and marvels*: the
corresponding phrase in Hebrew comes in Deut. 4: 34; 6:
22; Isa. 8: 18.

6. The text here reproduces the mood of ch. 2 (see 2: 2),
where the inadequacy of the 'wise men' is even more
emphasized.

8. *Daniel, who is called Belteshazzar after the name of my god*:
the name is here derived from Bel (= Marduk), the Babylonian god, but the name comes from Balatsu-usur (= 'may
he protect his life').

9. *chief of the magicians*: cp. 2: 48; 5: 11. *magicians* seems to
be a name given to embrace all kinds of wise men. *whom no
secret baffles*: for the reputation of Daniel cp. Ezek. 28: 3 –
'What? are you wiser than Danel [footnote: Daniel]? Is no
secret too dark for you?' *listen to the vision I saw*: unlike 2: 5,
where the king demanded both the dream and the interpretation, here it appears that Daniel is only asked to interpret the
dream which the king himself proceeds to describe.

10f. *I saw a tree*: the tree is a common symbol of life and
power. In Gen. 3, among the trees in the garden are 'the tree
of life' (Gen. 3: 22) and the tree which enables men to know
'both good and evil' (Gen. 3: 5). A fragment from among
the Dead Sea Scrolls refers to 'four trees' representing different
countries. The imagery there is parallel with some Iranian
texts which see the world as a tree with its trunk and branches,
and the branches stand for different ages of the world's
history. Perhaps the closest links are with Ezekiel who
compares Israel to a twig of cedar which was plucked by an
eagle and planted 'in a city of merchants', where it sprouted
and became a sprawling vine (see Ezek. 17: 3–6), and who
also speaks of the tall tree brought down and the low tree
raised up high (Ezek. 17: 22–4). In Ezek. 31 Pharaoh of Egypt
is reminded of the fate of Assyria which also had been like a
tall tree unrivalled for beauty and 'the envy of all the trees'
(Ezek. 31: 9); Pharaoh, in turn, is to be cut down because of

his pride: 'Because it grew so high and pushed its crown up through the foliage, and its pride mounted as it grew, therefore I...made an example of it as its wickedness deserved' (Ezek. 31: 10–11). We are reminded of the words of the Magnificat:

> he has brought down monarchs from their thrones,
> > but the humble have been lifted high (Luke 1: 52);

cp. the Song of Hannah in 1 Sam. 2: 1–10.

13. *As I was watching, there was a Watcher, a Holy One*: in the later development of angelology the 'watchers' became a special class of angel, but here the term seems to be the equivalent of 'angel'. The use of the epithet *Holy* does not point to any moral excellence, but indicates the celestial origin of the Watcher. The Septuagint uses the word *phulakes* (= guards), perhaps influenced by the Greek poet Hesiod who refers to two sets of watchers or guardians, the first consisting of the spirits of men of the 'golden age' in the primeval past. The Greek philosopher Plato (in the *Laws*) says that 'Chronos placed over our cities, as kings and rulers, not men but daemons of a more divine and excellent race.' In the development of ideas about angels, it was understood that each nation had its angel. The apocalyptic writing Enoch refers to them as the 'seventy shepherds' of the nations (Enoch 89: 59–76), whilst the apocryphal writing Ecclesiasticus says that God 'appointed a ruler' for every nation (17: 17). In Cave IV at Qumran one of the manuscripts containing Deut. 32: 8–9 reads:

> When the Most High parcelled out the nations...
> he laid down the boundaries of every people
> according to the number of the sons of God...

(this is the reading the N.E.B. has followed) and this text seems to have influenced the later theory that different 'sons of God' (= angels) were responsible for the nations (cp. Dan. 10: 13, 21; 12: 1). The growing emphasis on angels was due largely to the fact that God is seen as transcendent, 'high and exalted' (Isa. 6: 1), and the angels take on the role of intermediaries between God and his creation. At the same time, they are the bearers of his revelation. Cp. the function served by 'the angel of the LORD' in Zech. 1–6.

15. *tethered with an iron ring*: the meaning here is far from clear. The writer has moved from the imagery of the tree to the plight of the king himself, as the N.E.B. translation suggests. He is like an animal, tethered by an iron ring. The N.E.B. translation *let him eat his fill* is a conjectured rendering of a word commonly translated as 'bronze'. Many understood a reference to 'iron and bronze' as an indication of the rigour of the punishment which the king is to undergo. The N.E.B. translation points to the king living like an ox and feeding upon the lush grass.

16. *let his mind cease to be a man's mind*: the word translated *cease to be* is one that probably indicated a form of mental derangement.

17. The *Watchers* are here described as passing the sentence on Nebuchadnezzar, and some commentators see in this a Babylonian belief in the rule of the world by fate. The verse goes on, however, to assert that *the Most High is sovereign* and Daniel, in his interpretation of the dream, refers to the decree as being one passed by God and not the watchers (see verse 24).

19. *Daniel...was dumbfounded*: this is not the only occasion when Daniel is described as deeply moved by the divine revelation. Elsewhere he is almost at the point of fainting in the presence of the divine glory (see 8: 17–18; 10: 8–10 and compare what is said of John in Rev. 1: 17–18).

19–23. Daniel proceeds to recapitulate the elements of the dream and apply them to Nebuchadnezzar's situation. The way in which the dream is repeated almost suggests that, in one form of the story, as in ch. 2, the king had asked for the contents of the dream as well as its interpretation.

25. *you will have to live with the wild beasts*: the mania here mentioned is called zoanthropy, in which a human being

imagines himself to be an animal. The punishment is to persist until the king is repentant and recognizes the divine authority. Daniel does not deny a place to human authority; it is essential, however, that that authority should be seen as derived from God and not self-derived. God *gives it* (i.e. the kingship) *to whom he will.*

26f. Daniel even suggests that the threatened disaster can be averted. The stump is still present and so restoration, too, is possible, but the king, for his part, must *acknowledge the sovereignty of heaven* (heaven for the first time in the Old Testament being used as the equivalent of God) and indicate by his actions his change of heart. The word translated *charity* is 'righteousness', and in this context it obviously refers to 'good works' or 'almsgiving'. Whilst the king is called upon to acknowledge God's sovereignty, it is not anticipated that he will actually become a Jew, and accordingly the only demands upon him can be moral ones. It is as though he is told that

> The eyes of the LORD are upon the righteous,
> and his ears are open to their cries (Ps. 34: 15),

but that this is only possible if he is ready to 'turn from evil and do good' (Ps. 34: 14). Charity is seen as the application of righteousness to the situation of the poor and oppressed. There is no suggestion that this is all that righteousness involves. Because prophets like Amos had seen neglect of the poor as one of the ways in which Israelites had failed to live in accordance with the righteousness of God (see Amos 2: 6-7; 3: 15), attention to the needs of the poor and *wretched* became for later Jews the chief way of showing the virtue of righteousness. In the New Testament, too, Dorcas is commended for her charities (Acts 9: 36), whilst Cornelius, apart from his prayers, is chiefly commended for his public charity (Acts 10: 2). ✶

THE SENTENCE IS PASSED

28, 29 All this befell King Nebuchadnezzar. At the end of
twelve months the king was walking on the roof of the
30 royal palace at Babylon, and he exclaimed, 'Is not this
Babylon the great which I have built as a royal residence
by my own mighty power and for the honour of my
31 majesty?' The words were still on his lips, when a voice
came down from heaven: 'To you, King Nebuchadnezzar, the word is spoken: the kingdom has passed from
32 you. You are banished from the society of men and you
shall live with the wild beasts; you shall feed on grass like
oxen, and seven times will pass over you until you have
learnt that the Most High is sovereign over the kingdom
33 of men and gives it to whom he will.' At that very moment
this judgement came upon Nebuchadnezzar. He was
banished from the society of men and ate grass like oxen;
his body was drenched by the dew of heaven, until his hair
grew long like goats' hair and his nails like eagles' talons.[a]

✻ The king is given his year's stay of sentence, but, instead
of humbling himself before God, is shown as glorying in
his own efforts. No sooner is the proud boast off his lips
than the divine judgement falls. Only through experience can
he learn the truth of men's limitations. The details of the divine
decree, foreshadowed in the dream and already interpreted by
Daniel, are seen as taking place. There is also the added feature
that 'his hair grew long like goats' hair and his nails like
eagles' talons' (verse 33).

28–30. The way in which the scene is set admirably fits in

[a] goats' hair...eagles' talons: *prob. rdg.; Aram.* eagles' and his nails
like birds'.

with what we know of Nebuchadnezzar's Babylon. An inscription refers to the palace as 'the seat of my royalty' and as 'the dwelling of joy and rejoicing'. It is spoken of in another as a 'brilliant place' and 'the abode of majesty in Babylon'. The reputation of the splendour of the rebuilt city continued and the book of Revelation sees it as the representative image of a great city (see Rev. 14: 8; 16: 19).

31. *a voice came down*: this heavenly voice was called by the later Jews a *bath-qol*, 'a daughter of a voice'. We have an illustration of it in the story of Jesus' baptism (see Matt. 3: 17). Earlier, in the prophets, there is reference to the divine word issuing, as it were, from the divine council chamber (cp. Isa. 9: 8).

33. *his nails like eagles' talons*: many commentators see a parallel in *The Story of Ahikar*, a popular romance, discovered among other Aramaic documents at Elephantine (an island on the Nile), where there was a Jewish colony late in the fifth century B.C. It had been previously known in a number of translations, and influenced Aesop's fables and many collections of proverbs and stories. Ahikar is described as an Assyrian official under Sennacherib, and it is possible that the book was Assyrian in origin. In the story Ahikar is made to say 'my nails were grown long like eagles''. There is also a similar reference to long finger-nails in the 'Babylonian Job', an Akkadian work which describes the sufferings and plight of a person similar to Job in the Old Testament. ✻

RESTORATION AND THANKSGIVING

At the end of the appointed time, I, Nebuchadnezzar, 34 raised my eyes to heaven and I returned to my right mind. I blessed the Most High, praising and glorifying the Ever-living One:

His sovereignty is never-ending
and his rule endures through all generations;

35 all dwellers upon earth count for nothing
and he deals as he wishes with the host of heaven;[a]
no one may lay hand upon him
and ask him what he does.

36 At that very time I returned to my right mind and my majesty and royal splendour were restored to me for the glory of my kingdom. My courtiers and my nobles sought audience of me. I was established in my kingdom
37 and my power was greatly increased. Now I, Nebuchadnezzar, praise and exalt and glorify the King of heaven; for all his acts are right and his ways are just and those whose conduct is arrogant he can bring low.

* The seven years pass, and the king is seen as acknowledging God and recovering from his madness. Self-glorification had reduced the king to the level of the bestial, but his recognition of divine sovereignty means his restoration to the regal dignity of a human being (verse 36) and the glorification of God is a fitting response.

34f. *I blessed the Most High*: to bless God is to acknowledge that all blessing comes from him (cp. Ps. 103: 2 – 'Bless the LORD, my soul, and forget none of his benefits.' The whole of this psalm conveys this sentiment). *the Ever-living One*: this phrase is translated in Dan. 12: 7 as 'him who lives for ever', but becomes a popular way of expressing God's being (cp. Ecclus. 18: 1; Rev. 4: 9–10; 5: 13; 10: 6). *His sovereignty is never-ending*: the language here echoes that of Ps. 145: 13 (a psalm already used in Dan. 4: 3). By comparison with God men count for nothing (cp. Isa. 40: 17). *the host of heaven*: can refer to the stars (cp. Deut. 4: 19; Jer. 33: 22) or to angelic beings (cp. 1 Kings 22: 19). It is possible that both are included

[a] *Prob. rdg.; Aram. adds* and the dwellers upon earth.

here, as the phrase is stressing God's celestial sovereignty alongside his terrestrial control.

37. The letter ends not in an ordinary greeting, but with a further doxology. It was natural for Nebuchadnezzar to speak of God as *King of heaven*, for the Babylonian god, Marduk, was often addressed as *King*. The Psalter, however, contains many references to Yahweh as king (cp. Ps. 47; 93: 1; 97: 1; 99: 1). ✴

Belshazzar's feast

THE JUDGEMENT ON SACRILEGE

BELSHAZZAR THE KING GAVE A BANQUET for a 5 thousand of his nobles and was drinking wine in the presence of the thousand. Warmed by the wine, he gave 2 orders to fetch the vessels of gold and silver which his father Nebuchadnezzar had taken from the sanctuary at Jerusalem, that he and his nobles, his concubines and his courtesans, might drink from them. So the vessels of gold and 3 silver*ᵃ* from the sanctuary in the house of God at Jerusalem were brought in, and the king and his nobles, his concubines and his courtesans, drank from them. They drank wine 4 and praised the gods of gold and silver, of bronze and iron, and of wood and stone. Suddenly there appeared 5 the fingers of a human hand writing on the plaster of the palace wall opposite the lamp, and the king could see the back of the hand as it wrote. At this the king's mind was 6 filled with dismay and he turned pale, he became limp in every limb and his knees knocked together. He called 7

[a] and silver: *so Theod.; Aram. om.*

loudly for the exorcists, Chaldaeans, and diviners to be
brought in; then, addressing the wise men of Babylon,
he said, 'Whoever can read this writing and tell me its
interpretation shall be robed in purple and honoured with
a chain of gold round his neck and shall rank as third in
8 the kingdom.' Then all the king's wise men came in, but
they could not read the writing or interpret it to the king.
9 King Belshazzar sat there pale and utterly dismayed, while
his nobles were perplexed.

10   The king and his nobles were talking when the queen
entered the banqueting-hall: 'Long live the king!'
she said. 'Why this dismay, and why do you look so
11 pale? There is a man in your kingdom who has in him
the spirit of the holy gods, a man who was known in
your father's time to have a clear understanding and
godlike wisdom. King Nebuchadnezzar, your father,
appointed him chief of the magicians, exorcists, Chald-
12 aeans, and diviners.*a* This same Daniel, whom the king
named Belteshazzar, is known to have a notable spirit,
with knowledge and understanding, and the gift of
interpreting dreams, explaining riddles and unbinding
spells;*b* let him be summoned now and he will give the
13 interpretation.' Daniel was then brought into the king's
presence and the king said to him, 'So you are Daniel,
one of the Jewish exiles whom the king my father
14 brought from Judah. I have heard that you possess the
spirit of the holy*c* gods and that you are a man of clear
15 understanding and peculiar wisdom. The wise men, the
exorcists, have just been brought into my presence to

[a] *So Theod.; Aram. adds* the king your father.
[b] *Or* and solving problems.   [c] *So some MSS.; others om.*

58

read this writing and tell me its interpretation, and they
have been unable to interpret it. But I have heard it said 16
of you that you are able to give interpretations and to
unbind spells.[a] So now, if you are able to read the words
and tell me what they mean, you shall be robed in purple
and honoured with a chain of gold round your neck and
shall rank as third in the kingdom.' Then Daniel answered 17
in the king's presence, 'Your gifts you may keep for
yourself; or else give your rewards to another. Nevertheless I will read the writing to your majesty and tell you
its interpretation. My lord king, the Most High God 18
gave your father Nebuchadnezzar a kingdom and power
and glory and majesty; and, because of this power which 19
he gave him, all peoples and nations of every language
trembled before him and were afraid. He put to death
whom he would and spared whom he would, he promoted them at will and at will degraded them. But, when 20
he became haughty, stubborn and presumptuous, he was
deposed from his royal throne and his glory was taken
from him. He was banished from the society of men, his 21
mind became like that of a beast, he had to live with the
wild asses and to eat grass like oxen, and his body was
drenched with the dew of heaven, until he came to know
that the Most High God is sovereign over the kingdom
of men and sets up over it whom he will. But you, his 22
son Belshazzar, did not humble your heart, although
you knew all this. You have set yourself up against the 23
Lord of heaven. The vessels of his temple have been
brought to your table; and you, your nobles, your
concubines, and your courtesans have drunk from them.

[a] *Or* and to solve problems.

You have praised the gods of silver and gold, of bronze and iron, of wood and stone, which neither see nor hear nor know, and you have not given glory to God, in whose charge is your very breath and in whose hands are all
24 your ways. This is why that hand was sent from his very
25 presence and why it wrote this inscription. And these are the words of the writing which was inscribed: *Mene*
26 *mene tekel u-pharsin.* Here is the interpretation: *mene:*[a] God has numbered the days of your kingdom and brought
27 it to an end; *tekel:*[b] you have been weighed in the balance
28 and found wanting; *u-pharsin:*[c] and your kingdom has
29 been divided and given to the Medes and Persians.' Then Belshazzar gave the order and Daniel was robed in purple and honoured with a chain of gold round his neck, and proclamation was made that he should rank as third in the kingdom.
30   That very night Belshazzar king of the Chaldaeans
31[d] was slain, and Darius the Mede took the kingdom, being then sixty-two years old.

* This chapter applies the lessons to be learnt from the end of the Neo-Babylonian Empire to the situation of pious Jews during the time of Greek domination. Belshazzar is represented as the son and successor of Nebuchadnezzar (see note on verse 1), but he has not learned from Nebuchadnezzar's experience. He commits the act of *hubris* (over-weening pride) in using for his own pleasures the vessels that had been brought from the temple in Jerusalem. A mysterious message announces his doom and revelry gives way to alarm. Daniel

[a] *That is* numbered.   [b] *That is* shekel *or* weight.
[c] *Prob. rdg.; Aram.* pheres. *There is a play on three possible meanings:* halves *or* divisions *or* Persians.   [d] *6:1 in Aram.*

is brought in and interprets it as a declaration of the imminent overthrow of the Babylonian Empire. The chapter presupposes the material we have in chs. 1 and 4, and its message follows the pattern of ch. 4 in particular. Earthly rulers, we are taught, cannot go unpunished, if they act in complete disregard of what is sacred.

1. *Belshazzar the king*: Belshazzar (= O Bel, protect the king) was not king in the fullest sense (despite Dan. 7: 1; 8:1 which number the years of his reign), although he became co-regent with his father Nabonidus, when the latter left Babylon for Teima. There exist two legal documents dating to 543 and 542 B.C., which record oaths sworn by the life of Nabonidus (*Nabuna'id*) and of Belshazzar (*Bel-šor-uṣur*) the crown prince. We have evidence that the annual New Year festival, which required the presence of the king as the chief participant in the cultic drama, was not held for many years, so that Belshazzar could not have been regarded as king. The New Year festival was held in 539 B.C., when Nabonidus returned to the city. *gave a banquet*: a later tradition of the capture of Babylon speaks of a night attack during a feast (Herodotus, *History* I. 191; Xenophon, *Cyropaedia* VII. 5), but it is likely that there is confusion with the New Year festival celebrated on Nabonidus' return to the city in 539 B.C. As Daniel tells the story, the occasion is an ordinary banquet and not a festival, although it would have been usual to pour out libations to the different deities, mentioning them one by one (see 5: 4).

2. *the vessels...from the sanctuary at Jerusalem*: with the temple destroyed the vessels were the only relics of the ancient Jewish cultus and so especially revered by the Jews (cp. Ezra 1: 7-8; Isa. 52: 11). The vessels are here regarded as preserved in their original form, whereas 2 Kings 25: 15 suggests that the vessels were melted down into their respective metals. The N.E.B. translation *Warmed by the wine* suggests that the act of using the vessels was performed when he was drunk. The act of sacrilege would have been abhorrent

even to non-Jews. The Babylonian Talmud (a sixth-century
A.D. Jewish commentary on the Law and other Jewish
traditions) says that the king knew the prophecy of
Jeremiah about Israel's restoration after seventy years of exile
(Jer. 25: 11–12; 29: 10) and, assuming that it had not been
fulfilled, brought out the vessels, believing that they would
not be needed any more for religious purposes in Jerusalem.

3. *his concubines and his courtesans*: the word translated
concubines normally conveys the meaning 'consorts' (cp. Neh.
2: 6, where it is used of the queen of Artaxerxes). As wives
did not usually attend feasts, the N.E.B. translation adds a
more lascivious note to the proceedings. Regular members of
the royal harem were absent, but the female entertainers are
regarded as present. (The Septuagint removes all reference
to women at the banquet both here and in 5: 23.)

5. *Suddenly there appeared the fingers of a human hand writing*:
the word *Suddenly* suggests that Yahweh's answer to the
king's effrontery was almost instantaneous. The word of
doom is duly written on the wall behind the royal seat,
where the lamp lit up the royal table.

6. *the king's mind was filled with dismay*: the verb translated
as *dismay* was used in 4: 5, 19 and occurs again in the queen's
speech (5: 10). Even the word translated *mind* is often used in
the context of anxiety or frustration (cp. Eccles. 1: 17; 2: 23;
4: 6).

7. *read this writing and tell me its interpretation*: even if the
words were written in an obscure form of Aramaic, it is
likely that the 'wise men' could read them. They failed,
however, to make any sense of the symbols. It is possible to
read the words and still not comprehend the significance; it
is almost as if you have a book and cannot open it (cp. Isa.
29: 11–12). *robed in purple*: purple clothing was a sign of
dignity among the Persians (Esther 8: 15; 1 Esdras 3: 6) and
the Seleucid rulers (1 Macc. 10: 20; 14: 43–4; 2 Macc. 4: 38).
The man clothed in purple would be regarded as royal (Song
of Songs 3: 10; Matt. 27: 28 – N.E.B. 'scarlet mantle').

The rewards offered are reminiscent of the story of Joseph (see Gen. 41: 37–44). *third in the kingdom*: elsewhere we have reference to 'three chief ministers', of whom Daniel was one (6: 2), but we have here a possible reference to Babylonian official titles. The king was head of the army, and his chief officer was one 'on his right', whilst the second was 'on his left'. The third was his adjutant (i.e. the confidential adviser). Some see the reference to *third* as an indication that the writer knew that Belshazzar was only second to Nabonidus and that Daniel could therefore only rank third in the kingdom, but this is a somewhat pedestrian way of interpreting the text.

8. For the failure of the wise men cp. Gen. 41: 8; Dan. 2: 3–12.

10. *the queen entered*: as she speaks of his 'father's' time, it is commonly taken that the 'queen' was the queen-mother. She has been equated with Nitrocris, the widow or daughter of Nebuchadnezzar. Some try to justify the reference to Nebuchadnezzar as father to Belshazzar (verses 2, 11) by suggesting that Nabonidus, on becoming king, took either the widow or daughter of Nebuchadnezzar as his wife. Belshazzar could thus be regarded as the son or grandson of Nebuchadnezzar. It is most unlikely that he would have been the actual son of such a marriage, as Belshazzar was already an adult when his father came to the throne. Attempts to establish the historical accuracy of the account can lead to distorted interpretations of the story.

12. Daniel is introduced as having the ability to interpret *dreams*, explain *riddles* and unbind *spells*. For the first, like Joseph (Gen. 40–1), he is blessed with divine insight. The solving of riddles also required the divine gift of wisdom (see 1 Kings 10: 2f., where the queen of Sheba puts her riddles to Solomon, and Ecclus. 39, where the writer sings the fame of the riddle-solver). The word translated *spells* really indicates 'knots' and so it can refer to Daniel's ability to unloose any spells used by other magicians to bind people or it could indicate simply his ability to 'solve problems' (as the variant

translation suggests). *Belteshazzar* is here said to be the name given to Daniel by the king, whereas in ch. 1 the name is said to have been given by the king's official. *let him be summoned*: as in ch. 2 one would have assumed that Daniel would have been summoned along with all the other magicians, but in both cases his initial absence is a device to make his later appearance even more effective. He steps in when everyone else has failed.

13. *So you are Daniel*: Belshazzar speaks as if he does not know Daniel. Ch. 8 speaks of Daniel going about King Belshazzar's business (8: 27), and the 'king' would surely have known him by the end of his 'reign'. As we have seen in verse 12, this 'ignorance' is also part of the build-up. Daniel is not to be classed with ordinary officials; he is the only one who represents God.

17. Daniel refuses the gifts, but puts himself at the king's service. The refusal is probably rhetorical, as he later is seen as accepting what the king had offered (see verse 29).

18. The words echo the feeling of ch. 4 (see 4: 22, 36).

19. The language expressing the royal power is similar to that used by Cyrus in the so-called 'Cyrus Cylinder', a record of his conquests, inscribed on a clay barrel. Cyrus refers to the 'princes and governors' who 'bowed to him and kissed his feet' and 'worshipped his name'. He belongs to 'a family which always exercised kingship' and declares that 'Bel and Nebo want him as king to please their hearts'. The Old Testament often speaks against the consequences of pride (see Deut. 8: 14; Jer. 48: 29; Ezek. 31: 10).

23. After speaking of Nebuchadnezzar's fate (verse 21, as told in ch. 4), Daniel turns to Belshazzar's sins. Like Nebuchadnezzar he has exalted himself against God; he has committed sacrilege; he has worshipped idols and failed to honour the one, true God.

25f. Whereas the others cannot read the signs on the wall, they are clear to Daniel. He could both read the symbols and also apply them relevantly to the situation. The Septuagint omits the first use of *mene*, and we almost certainly have three weights, the *mina*, the *shekel* and the *half-shekel. u-pharsin* (= and two halves) points to the *pheres* ('divided piece'). Some see the weights as referring to Nebuchadnezzar, Belshazzar and the Medes and Persians, who are seen as dividing up the empire. Others think the reference is to the three Babylonian kings named in the Old Testament – Nebuchadnezzar, Evil-Merodach and Belshazzar. Although indicating weights, the words, at the same time, are interpreted as passing a political judgement – numbered, weighed, divided. The introduction of the Persians is due to the consonants of the Half-piece (PRS) being the same as those of the Persians. This kind of pun was popular among the Jews (cp. the pun between the word for 'almond tree' and 'watch' in Jer. 1: 11 as indicated in N.E.B. footnote).

27. The idea of human conduct being weighed in the balances appears also in Job 6: 2–3; Ps. 62: 9; Prov. 24: 12.

30f. The overthrow of Babylon fulfilled the prophetic expectation (see Isa. 21: 1–10; Jer. 51: 39, 47). *That very night Belshazzar...was slain*: the regular account of the capture of Babylon by the Persians asserts that the Persian forces occupied the city by night and that the populace eagerly welcomed them. There is no reference to Belshazzar's death, and we are told that Nabonidus was taken prisoner at a later date. The Persian forces were under the leadership of Gobryas (Gubaru) who subsequently served as governor of the city, acting for Cyrus. It is possible that Cyrus' son, Cambyses, who later succeeded his father as king, was also involved. By contrast, the book of Daniel refers to a Mede, Darius, as taking 'the kingdom'. Possibly influenced by the prophecies of Isaiah and Jeremiah, which had pointed to the Medes as overthrowing Babylon (see Isa. 13: 17; 21: 2; Jer. 51: 11, 28), the writer places a Median Empire between Babylon and Persia. The reference to Darius being *sixty-two years old* may be an attempt to indicate that there was only a brief interval before Persian sovereignty (but the Septuagint omits all reference to Darius' age). In any case, Darius is a Persian and not a Median name, and there is a possible confusion with the capture of Babylon by Darius I (who had become king in 521 B.C.) in 520 B.C. after an uprising. *

Daniel in the lions' pit

THE ROYAL DECREE AND DANIEL'S FAITH

6 IT PLEASED DARIUS TO APPOINT SATRAPS over the kingdom, a hundred and twenty in number in charge 2 of the whole kingdom, and over them three chief ministers, to whom the satraps should send reports so that the king's 3 interests might not suffer; of these three, Daniel was one. In the event Daniel outshone the other ministers and the satraps because of his ability, and the king had it in mind to 4 appoint him over the whole kingdom. Then the chief ministers and the satraps began to look round for some pretext to attack Daniel's administration of the kingdom, but they failed to find any malpractice on his part; for he 5 was faithful to his trust. Since they could discover no neglect of duty or malpractice, they said, 'There will be no charge to bring against this Daniel unless we find one 6 in his religion.' These chief ministers and satraps watched for an opportunity to approach the king, and said to him, 7 'Long live King Darius! All we, the ministers of the kingdom, prefects, satraps, courtiers, and viceroys, have taken counsel and agree that the king should issue a decree and bring an ordinance into force, that whoever within the next thirty days shall present a petition to any god or man other than the king shall be thrown into the lions' pit. Now, O king, issue the ordinance and have it 8 put in writing, so that it may be unalterable, for the law of the Medes and Persians stands for ever.' Accordingly 9 King Darius issued the ordinance in written form.

When Daniel learnt that this decree had been issued, he 10 went into his house. He had had windows made in his roof-chamber looking towards Jerusalem; and there he knelt down three times a day and offered prayers and praises to his God as his custom had always been. His 11 enemies watched for an opportunity to catch Daniel and found him at his prayers making supplication to his God. Then they came into the king's presence and reminded 12 him of the ordinance. 'Your majesty,' they said, 'have you not issued an ordinance that any person who, within the next thirty days, shall present a petition to any god or man other than your majesty shall be thrown into the lions' pit?' The king answered, 'Yes, it is fixed. The law of the Medes and Persians stands for ever.' So in the king's 13 presence they said, 'Daniel, one of the Jewish exiles, has ignored the ordinance issued by your majesty, and is making petition to his god three times a day.' When the 14 king heard this, he was greatly distressed. He tried to think of a way to save Daniel, and continued his efforts till sunset; then those same men watched for an oppor- 15 tunity to approach the king, and said to him, 'Your majesty must know that by the law of the Medes and Persians no ordinance or decree issued by the king may be altered.' So the king gave orders and Daniel was brought 16 and thrown into the lions' pit; but he said to Daniel, 'Your own God, whom you serve continually, will save

17 you.' A stone was brought and put over the mouth of the pit, and the king sealed it with his signet and with the signets of his nobles, so that no one might intervene to rescue Daniel.

✶ This story points to the favourable position given to Jews after the overthrow of the Babylonian Empire. Jewish success only causes the envy and malice of rivals. Daniel is described as apparently secure in the king's favour, and the only possible area of anti-Jewish activity had to be connected with religious practices. Jews will not compromise their faith, and the suggestion is therefore made that all religious practices apart from those ordered by the king should be temporarily discontinued. Daniel is shown as continuing his regular prayers. There is nothing vague about his witness; he is ready to give thanks in the middle of possible danger and persecution. The story is demonstrating that the man of faith must be prepared to live dangerously. As Jesus later put it: 'The man who tries to preserve his life will lose it' (see Matt. 16: 25). There are marked similarities to ch. 3. There the three friends witnessed to their faith in God; now Daniel (an old man of well over eighty, if one were to press the chronology of the book) has his time of trial. Nothing is said of the three here; there is no need to argue that they were dead by now, as the writer of the book is drawing upon a different tale. Some have supposed, as a background, a myth about a hero descending into the 'pit' of the underworld and returning to earth alive.

1f. *to appoint satraps*: the Persian Empire was actually divided into satrapies by Darius I (521–486 B.C.). Esther 1: 1 gives the number of satrapies (or provinces) as 127, whilst Herodotus gives the number in the time of Darius I as 20. Actual Persian inscriptions give a number between 20 and 30. Josephus increased the number to 360, supposing that each of the three *chief ministers* (verse 2) was in charge of 120. It is possible that the Jews reached the number *one hundred and twenty* by thinking of smaller divisions. *chief ministers*: the word used here does not occur elsewhere in the Old Testament and comes from the Persian word *sorah* which means 'chief'. The appointment by the king of a Jew to so influential position is an indication of the very liberal policy followed by Persia. (This is corroborated by stories in Ezra and Nehemiah.) We have no evidence of the Persians appointing three chief ministers over the whole country. It possibly reflects the presence of three officers within each satrapy.

4f. The fact that the other ministers and satraps try to discover some other malpractice, in order to accuse Daniel, indicates that they were motivated by envy rather than anti-Semitism. The attack on the religion is the result of their inability to discover another area of attack. *in his religion*: literally the Aramaic means 'the law of his God'. The word translated 'law' is not the usual Hebrew word *torah*, but is the Persian word *dath*, used of judicial sentence (see 2: 9) or royal decree (see 6: 8).

7. The suggestion that Darius himself became the object of worship would have been completely alien to the religion of the historical Darius. It reflects rather the hellenistic period, when both Seleucids and Ptolemies were seen as divine.

8. The *unalterable* character of *the law of the Medes and Persians* is also affirmed in Esther 1: 19; 8: 8. The Greek historian Diodorus tells a story about Darius III, how he repented of a sentence he had passed, but could do nothing about changing it, because the king's word, once promulgated, could not be broken.

10. There is no suggestion that Daniel deliberately tried to go against the law, but rather that he carried on his customary practice of prayer. There are scriptural references to the custom of praying towards Jerusalem (cp. 1 Kings 8: 35; Ps. 5: 7; 138: 2), but the exile will have intensified the practice. Muhammed originally prescibed that Muslims should follow the same practice; only after his clash with the Jews did he demand that they should pray towards Mecca. *he knelt down*:

this posture of prayer is mentioned in 1 Kings 8: 54; 2 Chron. 6: 13 and also in the New Testament (cp. Luke 22: 41; Acts 9: 40). In later times it was more common to stand for prayer and this is reflected in Matt. 6: 5 and Mark 11: 25. *three times a day*: this seems to have become the practice of Jews in the Diaspora (i.e. dispersed Jews outside Palestine) during the late Persian and Greek times. Ps. 55: 17 refers to prayer at 'Evening and morning and at noon', but Ps. 119: 164 refers to 'Seven times a day'. Dan. 9: 21 refers to Daniel praying 'at the hour of the evening sacrifice'.

11–14. The plot against Daniel duly succeeds, and Darius finds himself forced to condemn Daniel because of the immutable character of the legislation he had been tricked into passing. We may compare the attitude of Herod when he was forced to issue orders for the death of John the Baptist (Mark 6: 26).

15f. The enemies of Daniel are represented as insolently persisting in pushing the king's need to act in accordance with his own legislation. Daniel is brought to the pit, but the king is seen as expressing the hope (if not belief) that Daniel's faithfulness must be rewarded: *God...will save you.*

17. The den was sealed to prevent interference (cp. the sealing of Jesus' tomb in Matt. 27: 62–6). ✳

THE GREAT DELIVERANCE AND DARIUS' DECREE

18 The king went back to his palace and spent the night fasting; no woman was brought to him and sleep eluded
19 him. At dawn, as soon as it was light, he rose and went
20 in fear and trembling to the pit. When the king reached it, he called anxiously to Daniel, 'Daniel, servant of the living God, has your God whom you serve continually
21 been able to save you from the lions?' Then Daniel
22 answered, 'Long live the king! My God sent his angel to shut the lions' mouths so that they have done me no

injury, because in his judgement I was found innocent;[a] and moreover, O king, I had done you no injury.' The 23 king was overjoyed and gave orders that Daniel should be lifted out of the pit. So Daniel was lifted out and no trace of injury was found on him, because he had put his faith in his God. By order of the king Daniel's accusers 24 were brought and thrown into the lions' pit with their wives and children, and before they reached the floor of the pit the lions were upon them and crunched them up, bones and all.

Then King Darius wrote to all peoples and nations of 25 every language throughout the whole world: 'May your prosperity increase! I have issued a decree that in all 26 my royal domains men shall fear and reverence the God of Daniel;

for he is the living God, the everlasting,
whose kingly power shall not be weakened;
    whose sovereignty shall have no end –
a saviour, a deliverer, a worker of signs and wonders 27
    in heaven and on earth,
who has delivered Daniel from the power of the
    lions.'

So this Daniel prospered during the reigns of Darius 28 and Cyrus the Persian.

* The story next introduces us to the king's misery, which was not unmixed with faith, for he goes to the pit and calls out to Daniel, hoping for a response and half-believing that there would be one. Daniel responds and he is raised out

[a] in his judgement...innocent: *or* before him success was granted me.

unharmed, 'because he had put his faith in his God' (verse 23). The hero of the story has been saved and all that remains is for punishment to be meted out to opponents of the faith and for a universal recognition of Israel's God. He is twice described as 'the living God' (verses 20 and 26) and it is for this reason that he is known as 'a saviour, a deliverer' (verse 27). The parallels with the story of the blazing furnace in ch. 3 are clear throughout. Note that both these stories are mentioned in Heb. 11: 33–4 as examples of faith. The writer of Hebrews goes on to refer to the military exploits of the Maccabees as further examples of faith, thus linking the stories in Daniel with the Maccabaean age.

24. The accusers of Daniel suffer the fate they visualized for him, just as Haman was hanged on the gallows he constructed for Mordecai (Esther 9: 25). In both cases the law applying to malicious witnesses is followed: 'you shall treat him as he intended to treat his fellow '(Deut. 19: 19).

26f. The ending is similar to that in ch. 3. In the latter, however, religious tolerance is granted; here the king is demanding that the God of the Jews be revered by all. (Cp. 3: 29; 4: 1–3.)

28. The story is rounded off by reference to Daniel's continuing prosperity (cp. 1: 21). *

Daniel's visions

GOD'S TRIUMPH OVER THE FORCES OF CHAOS: (1) THE VISION

7 IN THE FIRST YEAR OF BELSHAZZAR king of Babylon, as Daniel lay on his bed, dreams and visions came into his head. Then he wrote down the dream, and here his account begins:

In my visions of the night I, Daniel, was gazing intently ₂ and I saw a great sea churned up by the four winds of heaven, and four huge beasts coming up out of the sea, ₃ each one different from the others. The first was like a ₄ lion but had an eagle's wings. I watched until its wings were plucked off and it was lifted from the ground and made to stand on two feet like a man; it was also given the mind of a man. Then I saw another, a second beast, ₅ like a bear. It was half crouching and had three ribs in its mouth, between its teeth. The command was given: 'Up, gorge yourself with flesh.' After this as I gazed I saw ₆ another, a beast like a leopard with four bird's wings on its back; this creature had four heads, and it was invested with sovereign power. Next in my visions of the night I ₇ saw a fourth beast, dreadful and grisly, exceedingly strong, with great iron teeth and bronze claws.[a] It crunched and devoured, and trampled underfoot all that was left. It differed from all the beasts which preceded it in having ten horns. While I was considering the horns I saw another ₈ horn, a little one, springing up among them, and three of the first horns were uprooted to make room for it. And in that horn were eyes like the eyes of a man, and a mouth that spoke proud words. I kept looking, and then ₉

thrones were set in place and one ancient in years
　　took his seat,
his robe was white as snow and the hair of his head
　　like cleanest wool.
Flames of fire were his throne and its wheels blazing
　　fire;

　　[a] and bronze claws: *prob. rdg., cp. verse 19; Aram. om.*

10   a flowing river of fire streamed out before him.[a]
    Thousands upon thousands served him
    and myriads upon myriads attended his presence.
    The court sat, and the books were opened.

11   Then because of the proud words that the horn was
speaking, I went on watching until the beast was killed
12 and its carcass destroyed: it was given to the flames. The
rest of the beasts, though deprived of their sovereignty,
13 were allowed to remain alive for a time and a season. I
was still watching in visions of the night and I saw one
like a man[b] coming with the clouds of heaven; he approached the Ancient in Years and was presented to him.
14 Sovereignty and glory and kingly power were given to
him, so that all people and nations of every language
should serve him; his sovereignty was to be an everlasting
sovereignty which should not pass away, and his kingly
power such as should never be impaired.

    ✻ This chapter may well be regarded as the most important
in the whole book. It certainly acts as a bridge between the
two main sections, sharing the language of chs. 2–6 and
hinting at the story of the image in ch. 2. It serves thus to
bring the earlier chapters and their interpretation into the
context of the historical crisis under Antiochus IV Epiphanes,
and, in doing this, gives a unity to the message of the book as
a whole. The chapter, however, shares the atmosphere of
chs. 8–12 in locating the chief action in heaven rather than
upon earth. What happens on earth is seen as the counterpart
of what is true in the courts of heaven.

    In ch. 2 we saw history depicted in terms of the four metals
which represented a succession of empires. God's control of

        [a] *Or* it.   [b] *Lit.* like a son of man.

history was seen both in his destruction of the image (man's own construction and thus man's attempt to construct history) and in the establishment of his own indestructible kingdom. Ch. 2 contained no specific reference to the reign of Antiochus Epiphanes, but ch. 7, whilst first looking at the empires through the symbolism of 'four huge beasts coming up out of the sea' (verse 3), concentrates on the 'horn, a little one' (verse 8), which 'spoke proud words'. 'One ancient in years' (verse 9) is, however, seated upon the throne of judgement and 'one like a man' is invested by him with 'everlasting sovereignty' (verses 13f.).

1. This is little more than a connecting verse which links the visions with the preceding stories. There seems to be no significance in the dating of the *first year* of Belshazzar, which would have been 553 B.C., the third year of Nabonidus, when Belshazzar was officially entrusted with the rule of Babylon.

2. *I saw a great sea churned up by the four winds of heaven*: the imagery points to the great ocean above the earth (cp. Gen. 7: 11), from which the flood waters came or the primeval choas, in which Tiamat, the dragon, dwelt. Both Isaiah and Jeremiah compare the clamour of the nations with the roaring of the seas (see Isa. 17: 12; Jer. 6: 23). *the four winds* (perhaps the four winds in the Babylonian creation epic) indicate the four areas of the earth and so express the involvement of the whole earth (cp. Zech. 2: 6; 6: 5). In the Babylonian creation epic the god Marduk is described as stationing the four winds to prevent the escape of Tiamat, the dragon of the deep.

3–6. *four huge beasts*: in the prophecy of Hosea the lion, leopard and bear all appeared to emphasize the action of God himself (Hos. 13: 7–8), but here the animals emerge from the sea (i.e. the chaos) and are opposed to the divine rule. Chaos is to be subjugated by the divine word (cp. Ps. 68: 30; 74: 18–19; Ezek. 29: 3–5). It is probable that contemporary readers would have quickly recognized what the symbols stood for. The lion was used as the heraldic symbol for Babylon, but it is doubtful whether the others had heraldic significance. Some see a link with Persian plastic art, whilst others would posit that the animals were zodiac signs representing areas of the earth. The lion would be Babylon in the south, the bear Media to the north, the leopard Persia to the east, and the unidentified fourth beast Greece to the west. Nebuchadnezzar was described as a lion (see Jer. 4: 7; 49: 19; 50: 17) and his armies as eagles (or vultures) (see Jer. 49: 22; Ezek. 17: 3). Both the winged lion and the lion without wings and partly human occur in Mesopotamian art. In the case of the bear, the text simply indicates its readiness to attack and its voraciousness. We have no example in plastic arts of the leopard with four wings and four heads. The fourth beast is seen as even more dangerous and more frightful. The writer concentrates on this beast, because it is not his intention to give a survey of history. All history is seen as man's attempt to assert himself and yet, at the same time, it is under God's ultimate control. The writer is most interested in his own time, and the fourth beast is dealt with more fully, because it represents the actual ruling empire at the time of the composition of the chapter.

7. *horns*: it is noticeable that the first Seleucid rulers had their coins decorated with horns, the symbols of their royal power. The *ten horns* represent the Seleucid rulers up to the time of Antiochus IV Epiphanes. In order to get to the number ten, it may be necessary to include Alexander the Great and the two sons of Seleucus IV, whom Antiochus superseded in gaining the throne. If we omit Alexander from the reckoning, it would be possible to include Heliodorus, the murderer of Seleucus IV, who temporarily seized power for himself. Perhaps the number is not to be taken literally, but as expressing a long line of rulers before the appearance of Antiochus IV.

8. The *little one* is Antiochus IV who usurps the throne for himself. With him comes the crisis of history and the expectation of the coming of the divine kingdom.

9. *ancient in years*: older translations almost regarded this

as a title. It speaks rather of the ultimate character of God's tribunal. The imagery probably comes from Canaanite mythology, in which El was regarded as an aged deity with grey hair. In Ugaritic texts Baal, the younger god, is described as the one who slew the dragon Itu and so gained victory over the sea, thus establishing his kingship. (In verses 13–14 the second figure is seen as the recipient of authority at the hands of the 'ancient in years' and this may reflect the ancient mythology preserved in the enthronement festival or New Year rites.) *Flames of fire were his throne*: the combination of 'throne' and 'fire' is unique. There are many references to the divine throne in the Old Testament (e.g. Isa. 6: 1; Ezek. 1: 26; 10: 1) and to the fire which accompanies the appearance of God (see Exod. 3: 2; Lev. 9: 24; Deut. 4: 12). *its wheels blazing fire*: this possibly refers to the fiery top of the flaming throne, but may indicate the ornamentation of the throne (cp. the description of Solomon's throne in 1 Kings 10: 19).

10. *Thousands upon thousands served him*: for the heavenly court cp. 1 Kings 22: 19; Job 1: 6; Isa. 6: 1f. We have reference to the entourage of Yahweh in Deut. 33: 2; 1 Kings 22: 19; Ps. 68: 18.

the books were opened: the idea that human deeds were recorded was linked with the notion of God as the righteous judge (see Ps. 69: 28; Isa. 65: 6; Mal. 3: 16).

13. *one like a man* [cp. footnote: lit. 'like a son of man'] *coming with the clouds of heaven*: this is probably the most crucial verse in the whole book, and the most difficult to interpret with certainty. The phrase 'son of man' was later used as a title by the author of Enoch, an apocalyptic writing, and is found in the Synoptic Gospels as the title used by Jesus of himself. How are we to understand the reference here? There are three main lines of interpretation:

(1) Just as we have had reference to the beasts – an indication that 'the mind of a beast' (Dan. 4: 16) replaces the human mind, as man seeks his own self-glorification – so now the human figure stands for man as he is meant to be in the

77

divine intention. Man is 'in the image of God' (Gen. 1: 27)
and so is contrasted with the beasts. But the human figure is
equated with the 'saints of the Most High' (i.e. Israel) in
verses 18, 25 and 27, who are regarded as heirs of the universal
authority granted to Adam (Gen. 1: 28). It is in exercising
this authority over the earth that the 'image' is to be seen,
for man then shares in God's own kingship and sovereignty.
Israel, as the chosen people, is seen as the people through
whom the divine intention in creation is to be fulfilled. The
disobedience of Adam (see Gen. 3) had led to disaster and
frustration and this is contrasted with the obedience of the
loyal remnant. According to this interpretation the *one like* a
man is understood to be ascending to heaven to receive the
kingship from God's hands. Whilst the beasts, representing
powers hostile to God, rise from the sea, the human figure,
who is heir to the promises made to Adam, comes *with the
clouds of heaven.*

(2) The figure is seen as the Messiah, a heavenly being in
human form who receives from God a delegated authority.
The emphasis would be on the supernatural – with the clouds
indicating the realm of the transcendent. Just as the Psalms
and Deutero-Isaiah brought the language of creation and
redemption together by combining the imagery of the overthrow of chaos in God's creative activity with that of God's
deliverance from Egypt, so here Yahweh's victory over
Israel's enemies and the restoration of Israel are described in
the language of creation mythology. In Enoch the son of
man is a messianic figure, pre-existent, heavenly and majestic.

(3) The figure is seen as an angel, the heavenly counterpart
to Israel. Angels are often described as men (see Gen. 18: 2;
Josh. 5: 13; Judg. 6: 22; 13: 16). In the book of Daniel,
Gabriel is described as having 'the semblance of a man' (8:
15) or simply as 'the man Gabriel' (9: 21). Michael is said
to be 'your prince' (11: 1) and so opposes the angelic being
who is designated 'the prince of Persia' (10: 20; cp. 10: 13).
According to this interpretation, the 'saints' would also be

seen as angelic beings ('holy ones') (see verses 18, 25 and 27).

It seems better to see the imagery speaking of a descent rather than an ascent and to see an emphasis on the supernatural, but, like the book of Revelation which sees a conflict in the heavenly area as decisive for what happens on earth, so Daniel probably sees the heavenly man as the guarantor of the dignity which man is to show on earth, and the heavenly man (or angelic being) is the guarantor of the promise to Israel that she will fulfil her divine destiny ✻

GOD'S TRIUMPH OVER THE FORCES OF CHAOS: (2) THE VISION INTERPRETED

My spirit within me was troubled, and, dismayed by 15 the visions which came into my head, I, Daniel, approa- 16 ched one of those who stood there and inquired from him what all this meant; and he told me the interpretation. 'These great beasts, four in number,' he said, 'are four 17 kingdoms*a* which shall rise from the ground. But the 18 saints*b* of the Most High shall receive the kingly power and shall retain it for ever, for ever and ever.' Then I 19 desired to know what the fourth beast meant, the beast that was different from all the others, very dreadful with its iron teeth and bronze claws, crunching and devouring and trampling underfoot all that was left. I desired also 20 to know about the ten horns on its head and the other horn which sprang up and at whose coming three of them fell – the horn that had eyes and a mouth speaking proud words and appeared larger than the others. As I still 21 watched, that horn was waging war with the saints and overcoming them until the Ancient in Years came. Then 22 judgement was given in favour of the saints of the Most

[a] So Sept.; *Aram.* kings. [b] *Or* holy ones.

High, and the time came when the saints gained possession

23 of the kingly power. He gave me this answer: 'The fourth beast signifies a fourth kingdom which shall appear upon earth. It shall differ from the other kingdoms and shall

24 devour the whole earth, tread it down and crush it. The ten horns signify the appearance of ten kings in this kingdom, after whom another king shall arise, differing from his predecessors; and he shall bring low three kings.

25 He shall hurl defiance at the Most High and shall wear down the saints of the Most High. He shall plan to alter the customary times and law; and the saints shall be delivered into his power for a time and times and half a

26 time. Then the court shall sit, and he shall be deprived of his sovereignty, so that in the end it may be destroyed

27 and abolished. The kingly power, sovereignty, and greatness of all the kingdoms under heaven shall be given to the people of the saints of the Most High. Their kingly power is an everlasting power and all sovereignties shall serve them and obey them.'

28 Here the account ends. As for me, Daniel, my thoughts dismayed me greatly and I turned pale; and I kept these things in my mind.

* From here the pattern of the concluding chpaters is established. Daniel is granted God's revelation in the form of visions, but the interpretation is not self-evident. Only one of those present in the divine council-chamber can give the interpretation (verse 16). The interpretation speaks of the ruler who was 'waging war with the saints' (verse 21) and who even sought to assault the very heights of heaven (verse 25). He will be 'deprived of his sovereignty' (verse 26) and in his place there will be the universal and everlasting

reign of the 'saints of the Most High' (verses 18, 25 and 27). Readers would easily have identified the former figure with Antiochus Epiphanes and the latter with Israel.

15–16. Whereas, in the earlier stories, Daniel had been the 'wise man' capable of interpreting dreams and visions, the role is now reversed and Daniel must supplicate for an interpretation of the vision.

17–20. First of all, the beasts are described as figuring earthly kingdoms, whilst the 'saints' are given a heavenly and abiding kingdom.

21. The reference here is to Antiochus' attempt to stamp out Judaism. The situation seemed hopeless, but, in faith, the vision speaks of the persecuted as rejoicing.

25. *He shall plan to alter the customary times and law*: many commentators assume that, under Antiochus IV, the lunar calendar was introduced, whereas the Jews, in their religious rites after the exile, had followed a solar calendar. A change in calendar would involve a change in the times of festivals. As he had been a hostage at Rome for many years, it is suggested that Antiochus desired to follow Roman patterns. Accordingly not only did the king reorganize the Syrian pantheon, combining the worship of Ba'al Shamem (identified with Zeus Olympios) and Melcarth (identified with Hercules), but he also laid emphasis on the winter solstice in place of the equinoctial days, introducing a feast which coincided with the Roman Saturnalia. It is thought that the king would have enacted the major role in the cultic drama and so gained the title Epiphanes (= God manifest). It is possible, however, that the writer simply wishes to say that the king desired to take control of the heavens and outdo God in his governance of the seasons and natural processes. In defence of the earlier interpretation it should be pointed out that the Qumran documents indicate a rigid adherence to the time of appointed festivals. The community at Qumran, which used a solar calendar, pledged itself neither to advance the time nor postpone any of the fixed festivals. *a time and times and*

half a time: this is understood as indicating three and a half years (cp. 9: 27; 12: 7, 11–12). Perhaps the time was to be reckoned from the desecration of the temple. The actual time from the desecration of the temple to its rededication was three years and ten days.

27. *Their kingly power is an everlasting power*: the party of the *Ḥasidim* (= the pious) believed that, once the Jewish cultus was re-established, the great divine event which ushered in the final age would occur and that this act of God would be irreversible. ✳

THE VISION OF CONFLICT AND DANGER

8 1-2 *a*In the third year of the reign of King Belshazzar, while I was in Susa the capital city of the province of Elam, a vision appeared to me, Daniel, similar to my former vision. In this vision I was watching beside the 3 stream of the Ulai. I raised my eyes and there I saw a ram with two horns standing between me and the stream. The two horns were long, the one longer than the other, 4 growing up behind. I watched the ram butting west and north and south. No beasts could stand before it, no one could rescue from its power. It did what it liked, making 5 a display of its strength. While I pondered this, suddenly a he-goat came from the west skimming over the whole earth without touching the ground; it had a prominent 6 horn between its eyes. It approached the two-horned ram which I had seen standing between me and the stream 7 and rushed at it with impetuous force. I saw it advance on the ram, working itself into a fury against it, then strike the ram and break its two horns; the ram had no strength

[a] *Here the Hebrew text resumes (see note at 2:4).*

to resist. The he-goat flung it to the ground and trampled
on it, and there was no one to save the ram.

Then the he-goat made a great display of its strength. 8
Powerful as it was, its great horn snapped and in its place
there sprang out towards the four quarters of heaven four
prominent horns. Out of one of them there issued one 9
small horn, which made a prodigious show of strength
south and east and towards the fairest of all lands. It aspired 10
to be as great as the host of heaven, and it cast down to
the earth some of the host and some of the stars and trod
them underfoot. It aspired to be as great as the Prince of 11
the host, suppressed his regular offering and even threw
down his sanctuary. The heavenly hosts were delivered 12
up, and it raised itself*a* impiously against the regular
offering and threw true religion to the ground; in all that
it did it succeeded. I heard a holy one speaking and another 13
holy one answering him, whoever he was. The one said,
'For how long will the period of this vision last? How
long will the regular offering be suppressed,*b* how long
will impiety cause desolation,*c* and both the Holy Place
and the fairest of all lands*d* be given over to be trodden
down?' The answer came, 'For two thousand three 14
hundred evenings and mornings; then the Holy Place
shall emerge victorious.'

✳ With this chapter the language changes back to Hebrew
and the rest of the book is written in Hebrew. Most feel that
the literary style is decidedly inferior to that of the Aramaic

[a] and it raised itself: *prob. rdg.; Heb. om.*
[b] be suppressed: *so Sept.; Heb. om.*
[c] will impiety cause desolation: *prob. rdg.; Heb. obscure.*
[d] fairest of all lands: *prob. rdg., cp. verse 9; Heb.* host.

section. This suggests that the writer was much more at home in Aramaic than in Hebrew. There is also much more concern in these concluding chapters for actual history, and especially for contemporary history, with which the readers would have been familiar. The animal symbolism persists, but it is much more thinly veiled.

The battle between the twin-horned ram (representing the Medo-Persian Empire) and the he-goat (standing for Alexander the Great) recapitualtes the story of the conflict we had in ch. 7. The he-goat gives way rapidly to the 'four prominent horns' (verse 8), representing the four divisions of Alexander's Empire, but then interest is totally concentrated on the 'one small horn' (verse 9) – an obvious reference to Antiochus Epiphanes. There is a clear reference to his great act of desecration (not mentioned in ch. 7), whereby he 'threw true religion to the ground' (verse 12) and this outrage fills most of the next verses. In reply to the question about the duration of the suppression of the Jews, the answer is given that 'the Holy Place shall emerge victorious' after 1150 days (verse 14).

1f. Just as Ezekiel is described as being transported to Babylon from Jerusalem and as receiving his vision by the river Kebar (see Ezek 1: 1), so Daniel is transported in his vision to Susa, the Persian capital, where he receives his vision by the banks of the river Ulai. It is uncertain why there is a reference to the *third year of the reign of King Belshazzar* unless one assumes a knowledge that it was about that time that Cyrus gained a decisive victory over Astyages, the King of Media, and established a combined empire (about 550/549 B.C.). Perhaps the writer is simply saying that this vision was subsequent to that in ch. 7, which is dated to the first year of Belshazzar's reign (7: 1).

3f. *I saw a ram with two horns*: this indicates a knowledge of the combined Medo-Persian Empire, although elsewhere we have seen a tendency to think of Median and Persian empires as separate entities. The fact that one was longer than the other indicates the supremacy of Persia in the partnership and the longer duration of its control. The *butting west and north and south* is an indication of the expanse of the empire.

5. *a he-goat came from the west*: this clearly refers to Alexander the Great, and the word *skimming* points to the rapidity of his advance eastwards. Alexander crushed the might of Persia in a series of battles between 334 and 331 B.C. (cp. verse 7 'the ram had no strength to resist').

8. *its great horn snapped*: this refers to the early death of Alexander in 323 B.C. He was succeeded by *four prominent horns*, the kingdoms of Macedonia (including Greece), Asia Minor, Syria (incorporating the eastern portion of Alexander's empire) and Egypt. Syria came under the rule of the general Seleucus (and the rulers are therefore called Seleucids), while Egypt came under Ptolemy (after whom the Ptolemies are named).

9. *one small horn*: with this reference to Antiochus, we move into the writer's contemporary history. The campaigns of Antiochus to the *south* (i.e. against Egypt) took place in 169–168 B.C., and those eastward to recover territory lost to the Seleucid Empire began in 166 B.C. *the fairest of all lands* alludes to Palestine (cp. Ezek. 20: 6; Dan. 11: 16, 41).

10f. *It aspired to be as great as the Prince of the host*: this repeats the assertion that Antiochus tried to combat with God himself (see 7: 21, 25). Usually *the Prince of the host* would refer to an angelic being (cp. 12: 1), but, as the writer speaks of *his sanctuary*, it seems that Antiochus is seen as fighting with God himself. Antiochus desecrated the temple by setting up a heathen altar and by suppressing the regular sacrifices offered up twice daily.

12. *The heavenly hosts were delivered up*: the N.E.B. translation indicates the temporary success of Antiochus in suppressing Judaism. His attack on the worship on earth is seen as an attack on the heavenly regions (cp. Isa. 14: 13–14). Some commentators take the reference to be the overthrow of earthly hosts, but the poetic imagery demands that the combat should be

placed in the heavenly sphere. Ch. 10 also speaks of the struggle in the heavens.

13. *how long will impiety cause desolation*: there is a veiled reference to the heathen altar set up by Antiochus, called elsewhere 'the abominable thing that causes desolation' (11: 31; cp. 9: 27; 12: 11). It has been suggested that we have substitute words for the original title of Zeus Olympios – the Lord of Heaven (=*Ba'al Shāmēm*). *Ba'al* is changed to a word indicating impiety or abomination, whilst *Shāmēm* is changed to *Shōmēm* (= desolating). The root *Shmm* can also have the meaning of 'empty', and Antiochus' action is therefore seen as appalling the Jews and emptying the temple both of worshippers and the presence of Yahweh. Another derivation supposes the root to have the meaning 'to be mad' and we would then have reference to Antiochus as *Epimanes* (= the madman) instead of *Epiphanes* (= [god] manifest).

14. *two thousand three hundred evenings and mornings*: the days are numbered by the sacrifices, and the time roughly corresponds to the three and a half years mentioned in ch. 7 (see 7: 25). At 1 Macc. 1: 54 the desecration is dated to 15 Kislev 168 B.C. and at 1 Macc. 4: 52 the resumption of the true sacrifice is dated 25 Kislev 165 B.C. (i.e. three years and ten days). Dan. 12: 11–12 attempts to revise the period, because the re-dedication of the temple and reinstatement of the regular sacrifices had not yet meant the coming of the divine kingdom. ✲

THE INTERPRETATION OF THE VISION

15 All the while that I, Daniel, was seeing the vision, I was trying to understand it. Suddenly I saw standing
16 before me one with the semblance of a man; at the same time I heard a human voice calling to him across the bend of the Ulai, 'Gabriel, explain the vision to this man.'
17 He came up to where I was standing; I was seized with

terror at his approach and threw myself on my face. But
he said to me, 'Understand, O man: the vision points to the
time of the end.' When he spoke to me, I fell to the ground 18
in a trance; but he grasped me and made me stand up
where I was. And he said, 'I shall make known to you 19
what is to happen at the end of the wrath; for there is an
end to the appointed time. The two-horned ram which 20
you saw signifies the kings of Media and Persia, the he- 21
goat*ᵃ* is the kingdom*ᵇ* of the Greeks*ᶜ* and the great horn
on his forehead is the first king. As for the horn which 22
was snapped off and replaced by four horns: four kingdoms shall rise out of that nation, but not with power
comparable to his.

In the last days of those kingdoms,   23
   when their sin is at its height,
a king shall appear, harsh and grim, a master of
   stratagem.
His power shall be great,*ᵈ* he shall work havoc   24
   untold;
   he shall succeed in whatever he does.
He shall work havoc among great nations and upon
   a holy people.
His mind shall be ever active,   25
and he shall succeed in his crafty designs;
   he shall conjure up great plans
and, when they least expect it, work havoc on
   many.
He shall challenge even the Prince of princes

[a] he-goat: *so Sept.; Heb.* hairy he-goat.   [b] *Prob. rdg.; Heb.* king.
[c] *Heb.* Javan.   [d] *So Theod.; Heb. adds* and not with such power as his.

and be broken, but not by human hands.

26   This revelation which has been given
of the evenings and the mornings is true;
but you must keep the vision secret,
    for it points to days far ahead.'

27   As for me, Daniel, my strength failed me and I lay sick for a while. Then I rose and attended to the king's business. But I was perplexed by the revelation and no one could explain it.

  ✳ Once again Daniel is described as being perplexed by the vision, but a human figure beside him (cp. Ezek. 1: 26), to be identified with Gabriel (= man of God), is introduced, who explains that the vision belongs to the end-time, when God is to intervene in history. The appointed period of God's wrath is nearing its end (verse 17) and Antiochus, the final and most awful manifestation of wrath, will be overthrown (verse 25). Daniel is enjoined to keep the secret of the vision, as though the fulfilment was in the distant future. We have here the first example in the Old Testament of an angel being named (the only other one named being Michael – cp. 11: 1; 12: 1). The decoding of the vision is far more explicit than elsewhere in the book and no doubt is left about the identification of the animal symbols. Despite this, Daniel is still described as being uncertain of the meaning of the revelation (verse 27). There is an attempt to enshroud the outworking of history in as much mystery as possible.

  15. *one with the semblance of a man*: the human appearance of the angels is suggested here. Ezekiel, too, describes the celestial creatures as being 'in human form' (Ezek. 1: 5).

  16. *Gabriel, explain the vision to this man*: later, in the book of Enoch, Gabriel is described as one of the four (or seven) archangels. (In Luke 1, he announces the births of John the

Baptist and Jesus.) *man* expresses the subordinate position occupied by Daniel as creature. Similarly, in verse 17, he is addressed as *man* (literally 'son of man'), just as Ezekiel had been addressed (see Ezek. 2: 1; 3: 1).

17. *the vision points to the time of the end*: cp. Dan. 8: 19; Hab. 2: 3. The vision is seen as dealing with the final crisis in the world's history. As ch. 7 has already indicated, the temporal process will give place to God's eternal kingdom (see Dan. 7: 14, 18, 22, 27). The theme will recur in ch. 12 (12: 4, 9).

18. *I fell...in a trance*: the word translated *trance* indicates a loss of consciousness rather than a mystical experience. In Gen. 2: 21 God puts 'the man into a trance' (i.e. a deep sleep), and Jonah is described as 'sound asleep' (Jonah 1: 6). It is only when Gabriel touches Daniel that he regains consciousness (cp. Dan. 10: 10, 16, 18). The idea that man is overwhelmed by the revelation of God's plans occurs frequently in apocalyptic writings (cp. Rev. 1: 17).

19. *the end of the wrath*: the Hebrew word translated by *wrath* is almost exclusively used of God's wrath, which Israel and Judah had incurred as a result of their unfaithfulness to the covenant and their unreadiness to receive the message of the prophets. As a result God was understood as having 'stretched out his hand against them and struck them down' (Isa. 5: 25; cp. Song of Three 5–9). A particular manifestation of the wrath had been Israel's subjection to other nations. When this subjection persisted long after the exile, there arose the notion that the wrath would only come to an end at the point of God's final judgement and the re-establishment of Israel. The intense persecution under Antiochus suggested that here were the final 'labour pains' before the birth of the new age. Dan. 11: 36 suggests that the wrath is finally to end in Antiochus' reign.

20. *the kings of Media and Persia*: the word *kings* should be understood as 'kingdoms' (see 7: 17, where the Aramaic has 'kings', but the Septuagint translates it by 'kingdoms'). In

8: 21 the same Hebrew word is used to express kingdom and king.

21. The Hebrew word for Greece (*Javan*) is derived from the Greek word 'Ionian'. The Ionian Greeks lived mainly in Asia Minor, and it was through them that Assyria, Persia and Egypt first came into touch with Greek culture and trade. *the first king*: the reference here is to Alexander the Great (king of Macedon from 336 B.C. to 323 B.C.). He was to die without an heir who could succeed him. (He married the daughter of Darius III, the last of the Persian kings, but, in his death, he left only an infant son.)

22. *not with power comparable to his*: the four kingdoms into which Alexander's empire was divided did not actually embrace all the territory he had conquered. The writer soon turns to the one king of the Seleucid kingdom, in whom chief interest is to reside.

23–6. These verses are in poetic form and read more like a prophetic oracle.

23. *when their sin is at its height*: the Hebrew suggests that 'sinners' are allowed to go to their allotted limits, but the N.E.B. translation (following the Septuagint) points to the sins of the heathen reaching their climax under Antiochus. *harsh and grim*: the original text suggests the shamelessness of Antiochus and not simply the hardness of his actions (cp. Deut. 28: 50). *master of stratagem*: some understand the word *stratagem* (literally 'riddles') as indicating the ambiguous character of his pronouncements; he was, in other words, adept at political intrigue (cp. 11: 21).

24. The N.E.B. follows the Greek text of Theodotion (see *Theod.* in Footnotes to the N.E.B. Text, p. x), as the Hebrew addition 'and not with such power as his' is clearly a repetition of the phrase in verse 22 ('not with power comparable to his'). Both here and in the following verse, the Hebrew text is confused and the N.E.B. tends to paraphrase, following the Septuagint translation.

25. *the Prince of princes*: Antiochus is seen as challenging

God himself who is the Prince over the princes (i.e. the angels; cp. 8: 11). *not by human hands*: there is an echo of the story of the destruction of the image in ch. 2 (see 2: 34). According to the Greek historian Polybius, Antiochus died suddenly after an attack of madness at Tabae in Persia in 164 B.C.

26f. For the solemn affirmation of the truth of the vision cp. 10: 1; 11: 2; 12: 7. This type of reassurance of the authority of the message is followed by the writer of Revelation (see Rev. 21: 5; 22: 6, 8). *keep the vision secret*: as the vision claims to have been given in the time of Belshazzar, this explains why the revelation was only being made known in the time of Antiochus. (Contrast Rev. 22: 10, where the revelation is seen as having immediate application.)

27. *I was perplexed*: the word translated *perplexed* indicates being 'astonished' or 'appalled' rather than simply the inability to comprehend. *no one could explain it*: this seems to point to the matter of comprehension, although it is odd that the inexplicable character of the revelation should be emphasized, when a most lucid explanation seems to have been given. Some suggest that what was inexplicable was why the revelation should be kept secret for so long. ✻

THE APPROACHING END FORESHADOWED IN PROPHECY

In the first year of the reign of Darius son of Ahasuerus **9** (a Mede by birth, who was appointed king over the kingdom of the Chaldaeans) I, Daniel, was reading the 2 scriptures and reflecting on the seventy years which, according to the word of the LORD to the prophet Jeremiah, were to pass while Jerusalem lay in ruins. Then 3 I turned to the Lord God in earnest prayer and supplication with fasting and sackcloth and ashes. I prayed to the LORD 4 my God, making confession thus:

'Lord, thou great and terrible God who faithfully keepest the covenant with those who love thee and
5 observe thy commandments, we have sinned, we have done what was wrong and wicked; we have rebelled, we have turned our backs on thy commandments and thy
6 decrees. We have not listened to thy servants the prophets, who spoke in thy name to our kings and princes, to our
7 forefathers and to all the people of the land. O Lord, the right is on thy side; the shame, now as ever, belongs to us, the men of Judah and the citizens of Jerusalem, and to all the Israelites near and far in every land to which thou hast banished them for their treachery towards thee.
8 O Lord, the shame falls on us as on our kings, our princes and our forefathers; we have all sinned against thee.
9 Compassion and forgiveness belong to the Lord our God,
10 though we have rebelled against him. We have not obeyed the Lord our God, we have not conformed to the laws which he laid down for us through his servants
11 the prophets. All Israel has broken thy law and not obeyed thee, so that the curses set out in the law of Moses thy servant in the adjuration and the oath have rained down
12 upon us; for we have sinned against him. He has fulfilled all that he said about us and about our rulers, by bringing upon us and upon Jerusalem a calamity greater than has
13 ever happened in all the world. It was all foreshadowed in the law of Moses, this calamity which has come upon us; yet we have done nothing to propitiate the Lord our God; we have neither repented of our wrongful deeds
14 nor remembered that thou art true to thy word. The Lord has been biding his time and has now brought this calamity upon us. In all that he has done the Lord

our God has been right; yet we have not obeyed him.

'And now, O Lord our God who didst bring thy people 15
out of Egypt by a strong hand, winning for thyself a
name that lives on to this day, we have sinned, we have
done wrong. O Lord, by all thy saving deeds we beg 16
that thy wrath and anger may depart from Jerusalem,
thy city, thy holy hill; through our own sins and our
fathers' guilty deeds Jerusalem and thy people have
become a byword among all our neighbours. And now, 17
our God, listen to thy servant's prayer and supplication;
for thy own sake, O Lord,*a* make thy face shine upon
thy desolate sanctuary. Lend thy ear, O God, and hear, 18
open thine eyes and look upon our desolation and upon
the city that bears thy name; it is not by virtue of our
own saving acts but by thy great mercy that we present
our supplications before thee. O Lord, hear; O Lord, 19
forgive; O Lord, listen and act; for thy own sake do not
delay, O God, for thy city and thy people bear thy
name.'

Thus I was speaking and praying, confessing my 20
own sin and my people Israel's sin, and presenting my
supplication before the LORD my God on behalf of his
holy hill. While I was praying, the man Gabriel, whom 21
I had already seen in the vision, came close to*b* me at the
hour of the evening sacrifice, flying swiftly.*c* He spoke 22
clearly to me and said, 'Daniel, I have now come to
enlighten your understanding. As you were beginning 23
your supplications a word went forth; this I have come to

[a] for...O Lord: *so Theod.; Heb.* for the Lord's sake.
[b] *Or* touched.
[c] flying swiftly: *prob. rdg.; Heb.* thoroughly wearied.

pass on to you,[a] for you are a man greatly beloved. Con-
24 sider well the word, consider the vision: Seventy weeks
are marked out for your people and your holy city; then
rebellion shall be stopped,[b] sin brought to an end,[c]
iniquity expiated, everlasting right ushered in, vision and
prophecy[d] sealed, and the Most Holy Place anointed.
25 Know then and understand: from the time that the word
went forth that Jerusalem should be restored and rebuilt,
seven weeks shall pass till the appearance of one anointed,
a prince; then for sixty-two weeks it shall remain restored,
26 rebuilt with streets and conduits. At the critical time,
after the sixty-two weeks, one who is anointed shall be
removed with no one to take his part; and the horde of
an invading prince shall work havoc on city and sanctuary.
The end of it shall be a deluge, inevitable war with all its
27 horrors. He shall make a firm league with the mighty[e]
for one week; and, the week half spent, he shall put a
stop to sacrifice and offering. And in the train of these
abominations shall come an author of desolation; then,
in the end, what has been decreed concerning the desolation will be poured out.'

✻ Until the present chapter the writer has expressed his
conviction that the crisis brought upon the Jews by the
extremist policy of Antiochus Epiphanes is the final stage before
the ushering in of God's kingdom. The 'truth' has come
through 'visions'. Now scriptural authority forms the basis of
the expectation, not the literal meaning of scripture, but the
'inspired' reinterpretation. Daniel is shown as wanting to

[a] to you: *so Sept.; Heb. om.*   [b] *Or* restrained.   [c] *Or* sealed.
[d] *Lit.* prophet.   [e] *Or* many.

know the meaning of Jeremiah's prophecy, where he speaks of the return of the Jews from exile after seventy years (see Jer. 25: 11–12; 29: 10). The year is supposed to be the year of Babylon's fall and, therefore, the fulfilment or non-fulfilment of the prophecy is very much an issue. Already (in chs. 7 and 8) we have had a seeming projection of history, in which the Jews have been seen as still awaiting deliverance, and as Daniel awaits illumination a prayer is introduced in which Daniel first confesses the nation's sin and acknowledges its shame (verses 4–10), next accepts that the disasters experienced by the Jews have been in line with the dictates of the divine law (verses 11–14), and finally, requests that God should restore Israel once more (verses 15–19). The angel Gabriel then appears and interprets the 'seventy years' as 'seventy weeks' (verse 24) of seven years each (i.e. seven seventies), and the final week (i.e. seven years) is the crucial period, starting with the murder of Onias III, the high priest (described as the removal of 'one who is anointed' in verse 26) in 171 B.C. Half-way through this period has occurred the desecration of the temple, when Antiochus 'put a stop to sacrifice and offering' (verse 27). This attempt at interpreting numerical references in Old Testament prophecy has influenced many to use both Daniel and Revelation as if they provided mysterious charts of the future. The author, however, was already convinced that God would demonstrate his power on behalf of the persecuted Jews in the immediate future, and the reinterpretation of 'seventy years' as 'four hundred and ninety years' simply reinforced that conviction. Because the period of the exile had not led to a realization of all the prophets had foretold, it is felt that the exile is still continuing. This same theme marks subsequent literature as well (cp. 2 Esdras 12: 10–12). Juggling with numbers did not give rise to it, although the author does claim to understand the prophetic writings even better than the original writers themselves. He is nearer the point of fulfilment and so can enter more deeply into the true signifi-cance of the writings, as the future is unveiled by God.

1. *In the first year...of Darius*: the dating is appropriate for the dramatic setting of the chapter. Babylon has been over-thrown and the pious Jew would naturally be recalling the prophecies of Jeremiah. In 2 Chron. 36: 21–2 the return from exile is regarded as a fulfilment, although actually less than fifty years had elapsed since the fall of Jerusalem in 586 B.C. There is a reference there to a 'sabbath rest', an allusion to Lev. 25 and 26, where the sabbath is a seventh year (cp. Lev. 25: 4). *son of Ahasuerus*: *Ahasuerus* (= Xerxes) is a Persian name and we know of no Ahasuerus who had a son Darius. Darius I (521–486 B.C.) was the father of Xerxes (485–465 B.C.).

2. *the word of the LORD to the prophet Jeremiah*: some think that the reference to *seventy years* in Jer. 25: 11–12 and Jer. 29: 10 were inserted after the return from exile, and that the period covered begins with the fall of Jerusalem in 586 B.C. and ends with the dedication of the rebuilt temple in 516 B.C., but this assumes an exact period. This is the first use of the personal name of God (Yahweh) in the book of Daniel. It is used again in verse 4, being an appropriate way of addressing God in prayer, and subsequently in the rest of the prayer.

3–19. The prayer has much in common with other prayers we have in the Old Testament (cp. 1 Kings 8; Ezra 9; Neh. 9). Whilst some regard the prayer as an interpolation, arguing that the request for forgiveness and deliverance does not fit the context, as a request for illumination would be more suitable, the pattern of this chapter is similar to the others where peril has issued in rescue or the vision has been followed by an interpretation. Here the prayer takes the place of the dream or vision, and serves the same function. It is possible that it goes back to the time of the exile (showing, as it does, an understanding of history as reward and punishment), and was revived by the *Hasidim* (pious ones) in the time of Antiochus Epiphanes. As we have argued, Daniel reflects their standpoint; he is seen as the pious penitent. Among the documents found in Cave IV at Qumran, there is an old hasidic liturgy which incorporates penitential elements. The whole course of history from the beginning of the exile is seen as a time of judgement, but this period of expiation comes to an end with the time of persecution. (Cp. 11:33,35; 12: 3, 10, where the sins of the past are seen as the cause of the unprecedented sufferings of the present.)

3. *fasting*: this was regarded as a necessary discipline, if one was to receive revelations (cp. 10: 2–3) *sackcloth and ashes*: these were the traditional signs of mourning (see Neh. 9: 1; Esther 4: 1–3). They also indicated a feeling of penitence. Here they accompany the confession of sins.

4. *who faithfully keepest the covenant*: we have here a reference to *ḥesed* ('covenant-love') which binds God to the covenant. He will faithfully observe his side of the covenant and demands that Israel be also loyal (*ḥasid*). This loyalty to God in the covenant also meant a commitment to one's fellow Israelite.

6. *thy servants the prophets*: the prayer thinks of the prophets as sent by God to maintain the covenant relationship, but the people have not listened to their message (cp. Neh. 9: 32, 34; Jer. 26: 5; 29: 19).

7. *right is on thy side*: God has been true to his commitment to Israel, but the Jews, to their shame, have failed. They are in the wrong. *shame*: cp. Ps. 44: 15.

11. *the curses*: the reference is to the series of curses which were linked with disobedience to the law (Deut. 27: 15–26, further developed in Deut. 28: 15–68 and Lev. 26: 14–45).

13. *we have done nothing to propitiate the LORD our God*: the Hebrew word translated *propitiate* literally means 'sweeten the face' which, elsewhere, is used in the sense of 'flatter' (cp. Job 11: 19; Prov. 19: 6). The suggestion is that a reformed pattern of life would have turned aside God's judgement (cp. Dan. 4: 27). In place of punishment he would show favour.

15–19. In the final section of the prayer, an appeal is made to God's 'great mercy' (verse 18), seen pre-eminently in the exodus from Egypt. This appeal to the exodus was relevant during the exile, but it also encouraged Jews during the persecution of Antiochus. God's act of deliverance will not only free the Jews, but will be the vindication of his own reputation (verse 19).

17. *thy desolate sanctuary*: this probably meant originally the destruction of the temple in 586 B.C., but the second century B.C. reader would see it as a reference to the outrage on the sanctuary by Antiochus.

19. *O Lord, hear; O Lord, forgive; O Lord, listen and act*: this threefold petition has been called the *kyrie eleison* (= Lord, have mercy) of the Old Testament. Prayers of this nature became part of synagogue worship and eventually influenced the development of Christian worship.

21. *the man Gabriel*: once again Gabriel, the interpreter of the vision in ch. 8, appears. Emphasis is laid on his human appearance. *flying swiftly*: this translation follows the Septuagint. In 1 Chron. 21: 16 the angel of the Lord is said to be 'standing between earth and heaven'. The reference to *flying* expresses a similar mediatorial role; he is the bearer of the divine message.

24. *Seventy weeks*: the interpretation follows the idea of the sabbatical year in Lev. 25 (especially verse 8). The time is needed for the eradication of Israel's sin and the completion of the time of atonement. The new age will then be ushered in, involving everlasting right, the fulfilment of vision and prophecy, and the consecration of the temple (cp. Exod. 30: 26–8). The 490 years are divided into

(*a*) 7 weeks (49 years) – from 586 to 538 B.C.

(*b*) 62 weeks (434 years) – from the end of the exile to the murder of Onias III (538 to 171 B.C.)

(*c*) one week (= 7 years) – from 171 to 164 B.C., divided into two at the desecration of the temple in Kislev (December) 168 B.C.

The second period, of 434 years, is much greater than the actual years – only 367 years – but the precise length of the Persian period was not known to later Jewish writers.

25. *one anointed, a prince*: this may refer to Zerubbabel,
who was prominent in Jerusalem at the time of the return
from exile (see Hag. 1; Zech. 4), or to Joshua, the high priest
at the same time. *conduits*: this meaning of the Hebrew word
has been confirmed by its use in the Dead Sea Copper Scroll.

26. *At the critical time*: the time of Antiochus is seen as the
crisis which ushers in the end of the age of the exile. *one who
is anointed*: the reference is to Onias III, the high priest, who
had been ousted by his brother Jason in 175 B.C. and then
killed in 171 B.C. at the instigation of Menelaus, another
claimant to the high priesthood (cp. 2 Macc. 4: 7–8, 23–35).
shall work havoc: this is an obvious reference to the devastation
wrought by Antiochus Epiphanes.

27. The *league* was made by the king with the hellenizing
Jews. The centre of the week is marked by the cessation of
sacrifice and the appearance of the desolator (cp. 7: 25 for
the three and a half years).

these abominations: the reference is to an image of Zeus
Olympios which was set up in the temple as a mark of its
rededication to pagan worship. In addition to the image an
altar was also involved (cp. 1 Macc. 1: 54, 59). It has been
suggested that the image displayed features of the king himself, disguised with a beard, as some coins of the reign assimilate the image of the king to that of Zeus. For the expression
abominations cp. 8: 13; 11: 31; 12: 11. The phrase 'abomination
of desolation' caught the imagination of later writers, and
came to express any symbol which indicated the claim to
divine rights on the part of man. Cp. Matt. 24: 15; Mark 13:
14. *

HISTORY REACHES ITS CLIMAX:
(1) THE ANGELIC VISITOR

In the third year of Cyrus King of Persia a word was **10**
revealed to Daniel who had been given the name
Belteshazzar. Though this word was true, it cost

99

4033

him[a] much toil to understand it; nevertheless understanding came to him in the course of the vision.

2   In those days I, Daniel, mourned for three whole weeks.
3 I refrained from all choice food; no meat or wine passed
my lips, and I did not anoint myself until the three weeks
4 had gone by. On the twenty-fourth day of the first month,
I found myself on the bank of the great river, that is the
5 Tigris; I looked up and saw a man clothed in linen with
6 a belt of gold from Ophir[b] round his waist. His body
gleamed like topaz, his face shone like lightning, his
eyes flamed like torches, his arms and feet sparkled like
a disc of bronze; and when he spoke his voice sounded
7 like the voice of a multitude. I, Daniel, alone saw the
vision, while those who were near me did not see it, but
8 great fear fell upon them and they stole away, and I was
left alone gazing at this great vision. But my strength
left me; I became a sorry figure of a man, and retained
9 no strength. I heard the sound of his words and, when I
10 did so, I fell prone on the ground in a trance. Suddenly
a hand grasped me and pulled me up on to my hands and
11 knees. He said to me, 'Daniel, man greatly beloved,
attend to the words I am speaking to you and stand up
where you are, for I am now sent to you.' When he
12 addressed me, I stood up trembling and he said, 'Do not
be afraid, Daniel, for from the very first day that you
applied your mind to understand and to mortify yourself
before your God, your prayers have been heard, and I
13 have come in answer to them. But the angel prince of the
kingdom of Persia resisted me for twenty-one days, and
then, seeing that I had held out there, Michael, one of the

[a] him: *prob. rdg.; Heb. om.*   [b] *So some MSS.; others* Uphaz.

chief princes, came to help me against the prince[a] of the kingdom[b] of Persia. And I have come to explain to you 14 what will happen to your people in days to come; for this too is a vision for those days.'

While he spoke to me I hung my head and was struck 15 dumb. Suddenly one like a man touched my lips. Then I 16 opened my mouth to speak and addressed him as he stood before me: 'Sir, this has pierced me to the heart, and I retain no strength. How can my lord's servant presume 17 to talk with such as my lord, since my strength has failed me and no breath is left in me?' Then the figure touched 18 me again and restored my strength. He said, 'Do not be 19 afraid, man greatly beloved; all will be well with you. Be strong, be strong.' When he had spoken to me, I recovered strength and said, 'Speak, sir, for you have given me strength.' He said, 'Do you know why I have 20 come to you? I am first going back to fight with the prince of Persia, and, as soon as I have left, the prince of Greece[c] will appear: I have no ally on my side to help 21-**11** 1 and support me,[d] except Michael your prince.[e] However I will tell you what is written in the Book of Truth.

* Chs. 10–12 should be regarded as a single vision. In the third year of Cyrus' reign Daniel is seen as receiving the revelation of the future. After a sketchy account of Persian power and of Alexander's conquests interest will be centred in Seleucid power up to and including the reign of Antiochus Epiphanes, for it is there that history is to reach its climax. It is there that the divine kingdom is to supersede earthly

[a] prince: *so Sept.; Heb. om.*   [b] *So some MSS.; others* kings.
[c] *Heb.* Javan.   [d] me: *so Pesh.; Heb. obscure.*
[e] *Prob. rdg.; Heb. adds* and as for me, in the first year of Darius the Mede.

authorities, and the righteous will be assured of their share in that kingdom. This first section (10: 1 – 11: 1) provides the setting for the revelation which is to follow (11: 2 – 12: 4).

1. *In the third year of Cyrus*: the reason for the dating is uncertain. The selection of Cyrus' reign is due to the fact that the historical survey is to begin with Persia. Daniel is here introduced in the third person and the Babylonian name Belteshazzar is also used, the only usage in the second half of the book.

2f. Daniel is only able to receive the revelation after a great personal struggle and severe asceticism. In Ezra 8: 21 fasting is seen as a necessary preparation for receiving a revelation. The note of confession is also present (cp. Dan. 9: 3-4). *choice food* literally means 'bread of pleasantness' and is contrasted with the 'bread of affliction', eaten at Passover.

4. *On the twenty-fourth day of the first month*: the dating is significant. Early in the first month occur the two great feasts, Passover and Unleavened Bread (Exod. 12: 1–20), and they were associated with the deliverance of Israel from Egypt. Daniel is now to be told of the future destiny of Israel (10: 14). His three-week fast had included the period of the festival, and so the overtones of the Passover message are discernible in this context.

5f. *I looked up and saw a man*: the angel is here described as a man and the description largely follows the imagery in Ezekiel (cp. especially, Ezek. 1; 9: 2–3).

7. *I, Daniel, alone saw the vision*: the fact that his companions did not see it emphasizes the momentous character of Daniel's experience. Details from this vision are used to describe the glory of the risen Christ and the effect of the vision on John in Rev. 1: 14–17. There are parallels in the story of Paul's vision on the road to Damascus (cp. especially Acts 9: 7).

11. *man greatly beloved*: this affectionate language was used by Gabriel in 9: 23 (cp. 10: 19).

12f. The angel explains the delay in granting Daniel the revelation he requested in his prayers. There has been angelic opposition in heaven; *the angel prince of the kingdom of Persia resisted me*: each nation was thought to have its own patron angel, just as Michael was seen as Israel's (cp. 10: 21; 12: 1). According to Deut. 32: 8–9 God is seen as assigning to each nation its own subordinate deity, later identified with an angelic being (cp. Ps. 82), whilst Deut. 29: 26 says that Israel was not really in a position to worship other gods as they were not assigned to Israel. The opposition by the angel-representative of Persia points perhaps to the notion of celestial warfare (cp. 2 Macc. 5: 1–4). This is another way of asserting that the ultimate destiny of nations is determined not upon earth, but in heaven. The development of monotheistic thinking led to substitution of 'angels' for the earlier reference to 'deities'.

16. *one like a man touched my lips*: the phrase *one like a man* is taken from Ezekiel (Ezek. 1: 5, 10; 8: 2). For the touching of the lips cp. Isa. 6: 7; Jer. 1: 9. Daniel recovers his speech through the touch. One act of healing is not, however, sufficient to reassure Daniel; he needs to be touched again (10: 18).

19. *Be strong, be strong*: there is a hint here of the opening and closing formulae used in letters, but the language also recalls Deut. 31: 7, 23 and Josh. 1: 6, 7, 9, 18.

11: 1. *the Book of Truth*: perhaps a distinction should be drawn between the Book of Truth and 'the books' (Dan. 7: 10). Some draw parallels with the Babylonian 'Tablets of Fate', which are linked with the creation epic and the cultic drama which re-enacted creation at the New Year festival. There was a later Jewish tradition that the books were opened on New Year's Day, predicting the future, as foreknown in heaven. As a prelude to the historical narrative in 11: 2–39, the reference to the Book of Truth points to God's control of history. God is understood as having everything under his control. It is as if everything is written down in his record, both the past and the future. History must inevitably move in the direction of its divinely planned climax. Ps. 139

emphasizes that everything about a man is known to God (cp. Ps. 139: 14 – 'Thou knowest me through and through') and the writer of Daniel sees this as true of all mankind. ✳

HISTORY REACHES ITS CLIMAX:
(2) THE SCHEMES OF MEN

2 Here and now I will tell you what is true:

'Three more kings will appear in Persia, and the fourth will far surpass all the others in wealth; and when he has extended his power through his wealth, he will rouse the 3 whole world against the kingdom of Greece. Then there will appear a warrior king. He will rule a vast kingdom 4 and will do what he chooses. But as soon as he is established, his kingdom will be shattered and split up north, south, east and west. It will not pass to his descendants, nor will any of his successors have an empire like his; his kingdom will be torn up by the roots and given to 5 others as well as to them. Then the king of the south will become strong; but another of the captains will surpass 6 him in strength and win a greater kingdom. In due course the two will enter into a friendly alliance; to redress the balance the daughter of the king of the south will be given in marriage to the king of the north, but she will not maintain her influence and their line will not last. She and her escort, her child, and also her lord and 7 master, will all be the victims of foul play. Then another shoot from the same stock as hers will appear in his father's place, will penetrate the defences of the king of the north and enter his fortress, and will win a decisive victory over 8 his people. He will take back as booty to Egypt even the images of their gods cast in metal and their precious vessels of silver and gold. Then for some years he will refrain from attacking the king of the north. After that the king of the north will overrun the southern kingdom but will retreat to his own land. 9

'His sons will press on to assemble a great armed horde. One of them will sweep on and on like an irresistible flood. And after that he will press on as far as his enemy's stronghold. The king of the south, his anger roused, will march out to do battle with the king of the north who in turn, will raise a great horde, but it will be delivered into the hands of his enemy. When this horde has been captured, the victor will be elated and he will slaughter tens of thousands, yet he will not maintain his advantage. Then the king of the north will once more raise a horde even greater than the last and, when the years come round, will advance with a great army and a large baggage-train. During these times many will resist the king of the south, but some hotheads among your own people will rashly attempt to give substance to a vision and will come to disaster. Then the king of the north will come and throw up siege-ramps and capture a fortified town, and the forces of the south will not stand up to him; even the flower of their army will not be able to hold their ground. And so his adversary will do as he pleases and meet with no opposition. He will establish himself in the fairest of all lands and it will come wholly into his power. He will resolve to subjugate all the dominions of the king of the south; and he will come to fair terms with him,*a* and he will give him a young woman in marriage, for the destruction of the kingdom; but she will not persist nor 10 11 12 13 14 15 16 17

[a] and he...with him: *prob. rdg.; Heb. obscure.*

18 serve his purpose. Then he will turn to the coasts and islands and take many prisoners, but a foreign commander*a* will put an end to his challenge by wearing him down;*b*

19 thus he will throw back his challenge on to him. He will fall back upon his own strongholds; there he will come to disaster and be overthrown and be seen no more.

20 'He will be succeeded by one who will send out an officer with a royal escort to extort tribute; after a short time this king too will meet his end, yet neither openly nor in battle.

21 'A contemptible creature will succeed but will not be given recognition as king; yet he will seize the kingdom

22 by dissimulation and intrigue in time of peace. He will sweep away all forces of opposition as he advances, and

23 even the Prince of the Covenant will be broken. He will enter into fraudulent alliances and, although the people behind him are but few, he will rise to power and estab-

24 lish himself in time of peace. He will overrun the richest districts of the province and succeed in doing what his fathers and forefathers failed to do, distributing spoil, booty, and property to his followers. He will lay his plans against fortresses, but only for a time.

25 'He will rouse himself in all his strength and courage and lead a great army against the king of the south, but the king of the south will press the campaign against him with a very great and numerous army; yet the king of the south will not persist, for traitors will lay their plots.

26 Those who eat at his board will be his undoing; his army will be swept away, and many will fall on the field of

[a] Or consul or legate.
[b] by wearing him down: *prob. rdg.; Heb. obscure.*

battle. The two kings will be bent on mischief and, 27
sitting at the same table, they will lie to each other with
advantage to neither. Yet there will still be an end to the
appointed time. Then one will return home with a long 28
baggage-train, and with anger in his heart against the
Holy Covenant; he will work his will and return to his
own land.

'At the appointed time he will once more overrun the 29
south, but he will not succeed as he did before. Ships 30*a*
from the west*a* will sail against him, and he will receive a
rebuff.'

* The revelation given to Daniel is a survey of history, as it
affected the Jews, from the Persian period to the time of
Antiochus IV Epiphanes (175-164 B.C.). This is the first
prolonged attempt in the Bible to provide a consecutive
historical narrative. Much of the detail, however, is so veiled,
that our identification of events often depends on external
records. The starting point is the same as in the vision of the
ram and the he-goat (ch. 8). Ruler after ruler is seen as
coming on the stage of history. Men have their schemes;
empires are won and lost; there are rivalry, alliances and
deceit. The author, however, is not going to confine his
attention to the actions of men; he is more concerned with
the relation of God's activity to what men do on earth.

2. *Here and now*: this is the normal introduction to a letter
or speech and should possibly be seen as the beginning of the
survey proper. *Three more kings will appear in Persia*: it is
likely that the three are the successors of Cyrus, namely,
Cambyses, Darius I and Xerxes, thus excluding Pseudo-
Smerdis who held power for a few months before being crushed by Darius I. *the fourth*: this number takes Cyrus into account
and the reference fits what we know of Xerxes (485-465 B.C.),

[a] Ships from the west: *Heb.* Ships of Kittim; *Sept.* Romans.

who led an enormous host against Greece in campaigns of 480–479 B.C. Some, however, would identify the four with those Persian kings mentioned by name elsewhere in the Old Testament – Cyrus, Darius, Xerxes and Artaxerxes. The suggestion that the fourth is Darius III and that Darius I is omitted because of the confusion with 'Darius the Mede' is supported by Nehemiah (Neh. 12: 22) who refers to Darius III, but that king would hardly merit what is said about the fourth in the text.

3f. Alexander the Great is well described as *a warrior king*. Apart from reference to his *vast kingdom*, stretching, as it did, from Greece in the west to the Punjab in the east, interest is concentrated upon the consequences of his sudden death in 323 B.C. Four main kingdoms succeed his empires, but there will be *others as well* sharing in the spoils.

5. *the king of the south*: Egypt was the southernmost part of Alexander's empire and was secured by Ptolemy, one of his generals. The Ptolemies controlled Egypt till 30 B.C. *another of the captains*: the reference is to Seleucus who, in the division of the empire agreed upon between the generals in 321 B.C., received the satrapy of Babylonia. In 316 B.C. he fled to Ptolemy from Antigonus, who had begun as satrap of Phrygia, but then extended his control from the Mediterranean to Central Asia. Seleucus served under Ptolemy till 312 B.C., but then regained his old satrapy after defeating the son of Antigonus. He broke the power of Antigonus in 301 B.C. at the battle of Ipsus, in which Antigonus himself was killed. Subsequently he controlled an area from Asia Minor to the north-west frontier of India. Hence he is said to *surpass* Ptolemy *in strength*.

6. *a friendly alliance*: about 248 B.C. Ptolemy II gave his daughter Berenice in marriage to Antiochus II (grandson of Seleucus) on condition that he should divorce his wife Laodice and deprive his two sons by her of rights of succession. This verse goes on to allude to Laodice's revenge in procuring the murder of Berenice and her child.

7. *another shoot from the same stock as hers*: Ptolemy III (247–222 B.C.) sought to avenge the murder of his sister Berenice and invaded the Seleucid kingdom.

8. *even the images of their gods*: Jerome, a fourth-century A.D. Christian writer, says that Ptolemy took back to Egypt statues of the Egyptian gods carried off by Cambyses, and so earned the title *Euergetes* (the Benefactor).

9. In 240 B.C. Seleucus Callinicus, in turn, invaded Egypt, but sustained a defeat, being forced to *retreat to his own land*.

10. *His sons will press on*: the reference is to Seleucus Ceraunus (226–223 B.C.) and Antiochus III the Great (223–187 B.C.). The *stronghold* is probably Gaza, which was the strongest fortress of Palestine to the south. Up to this point Palestine had been subject to Egypt.

11. This verse refers to the battle at Raphia in 217 B.C., where Ptolemy inflicted a severe defeat on Antiochus III, re-annexing Palestine to Egypt.

13f. Antiochus III seized the opportunity to attack Egypt, when Ptolemy Philopator died in 203 B.C. He allied himself with Philip of Macedon for this purpose. It appears that some Jews took sides with Antiochus III, claiming prophetic support for their action (verse 14: *to give substance to a vision*).

15. The *fortified town* captured by Antiochus III was Sidon, where Scopas, Ptolemy's general, was taken captive in 198 B.C.

16. *He will establish himself in the fairest of all lands*: this refers to Antiochus' complete conquest of Palestine.

17. *he will give him a young woman in marriage*: Antiochus gave his daughter Cleopatra in marriage to Ptolemy V in 194/3 B.C., hoping thus to gain control of Egypt. He did not succeed, because Cleopatra encouraged her husband to strengthen his alliance with Rome.

18. In 197 B.C. Antiochus had first invaded Asia Minor and then crossed into Thrace. In 192 B.C. he effected a landing in Greece, but in 191 B.C. the *foreign commander* (the Roman general) routed his forces at Thermopylae. The next year he suffered a further devastating defeat at Magnesia.

19. *he will come to disaster*: in order to pay the vast fine imposed on him by Rome, Antiochus the Great retired east and tried to plunder the temple of Bel in Elymais. The inhabitants turned on him and killed him and his followers in 187 B.C.

20. Antiochus' successor was Seleucus IV (187–175 B.C.), remembered because of his attempt to plunder the temple treasures in Jerusalem (cp. 2 Macc. 3: 1–28). He was killed as the result of a conspiracy, led by Heliodorus, and so died *neither openly nor in battle*.

21. Antiochus Epiphanes is called *A contemptible creature*, and emphasis is laid on the fact that he had no real claim to the throne.

22. *the Prince of the Covenant* is Onias III, the Jewish high priest. He was removed from office in 175 B.C. and murdered in 171 B.C. (9: 26).

24. The munificence and prodigal generosity of Antiochus IV Epiphanes is mentioned also in 1 Macc. 3: 30.

He will lay his plans against fortresses: the Syrian king tried to gain control of Egypt (cp. 1 Macc. 1: 19), occupying Pelusium and other frontier towns.

27. *they will lie to each other*: when Antiochus IV defeated Ptolemy Philometor the Alexandrians put his brother on the throne under the title Ptolemy Physcon. Antiochus then pretended that he was acting in the interests of Philometor, whilst the latter pretended that he believed in the disinterestedness of Antiochus.

28. Antiochus ended his first Egyptian campaign with an attack on Jerusalem and on the Jewish religion, here called the *Holy Covenant*.

30. *Ships from the west*: the Hebrew has 'Ships of Kittim', but the reference is to Roman intervention. Whereas 1 Macc. 1: 1 uses the name Kittim as a title for the Greeks, the Qumran Commentary on Habakkuk follows Daniel in using it as the name of the Romans. The Septuagint actually uses 'Romans'. (See the footnote in the N.E.B.) The anti-Jewish persecution

which marks the next section was sparked off by the demand
from the Roman envoys that Antiochus should leave Egypt.
He could not go against Roman demands, but vented his
spite on the Jews. ✻

HISTORY REACHES ITS CLIMAX:
(3) THE PERSECUTION AND THE PERSECUTOR'S FATE

'He will turn and vent his fury against the Holy   30*b*
Covenant; on his way back he will take due note of those
who have forsaken it. Armed forces dispatched by him   31
will desecrate the sanctuary and the citadel and do away
with the regular offering. And there they will set up "the
abominable thing that causes desolation". He will win   32
over by plausible promises those who are ready to
condemn the covenant, but the people who are faithful
to their God will hold firm and fight back. Wise leaders   33
of the nation will give guidance to the common people;
yet for a while they will fall victims to fire and sword,
to captivity and pillage. But these victims will not want   34
for help, though small, even if many who join them are
insincere. Some of these leaders will themselves fall   35
victims for a time so that they may be tested, refined and
made shining white. Yet there will still be an end*a* to the
appointed time. The king will do what he chooses; he   36
will exalt and magnify himself above every god and
against the God of gods he will utter monstrous blas-
phemies. All will go well for him until the time of wrath
ends, for what is determined must be done. He will ignore   37
his ancestral gods, and the god beloved of women; to no
god will he pay heed but will exalt himself above them

[a] Yet...end: *prob. rdg.; Heb. has different word order.*

38 all. Instead he will honour the god of the citadel,*a* a god
unknown to his ancestors, with gold and silver, gems and
39 costly gifts. He will garrison his strongest fortresses with
aliens, the people of a foreign god. Those whom he
favours he will load with honour, putting them in office
over the common people and distributing land at a price.
40 'At the time of the end, he and the king of the south
will make feints at one another, and the king of the north
will come storming against him with chariots and cavalry
and many ships. He will overrun land after land, sweeping
41 over them like a flood, amongst them the fairest of all
lands, and tens of thousands shall fall victims. Yet all these
lands [including Edom and Moab and the remnant*b* of
42 the Ammonites] will survive his attack. He will reach
43 out to land after land, and Egypt will not escape. He will
gain control of her hidden stores of gold and silver and
of all her treasures; Libyans and Cushites will follow in
44 his train. Then rumours from east and north will alarm
him, and he will depart in a great rage to destroy and to
45 exterminate many. He will pitch his royal pavilion
between the sea and the holy hill, the fairest of all hills;
and he will meet his end with no one to help him.'

* The narrative now turns to Antiochus' fury against the
Holy Covenant (verse 30*b*), his desecration of the temple
(verse 31) and his challenge to God himself (verse 36). From
verse 40 we move from historical narrative to the realm of
expectation and prediction. It is assumed that he will make a
further attack on Egypt (verses 40–2) and perish in Palestine,
the place where he has committed his greatest atrocities.
    31. The *citadel* probably refers to the temple itself. The

[a] *Lit.* fortresses.   [b] *So Pesh.; Heb.* beginning.

daily sacrifice was suspended (cp. 9: 27) and '*the abominable thing that causes desolation*' (obviously a statue of Zeus) set up.

32. We have a clear reference to two parties among the Jews – the hellenizers, ready even for apostasy, and the faithful (cp. 1 Macc. 1: 11–15). It would be wrong, however, to suppose that all hellenizers wished to abandon Judaism. Like the author of the First Book of Maccabees, the writer of Daniel sees the issues as very clear-cut. He will not allow a mediating position.

33. *Wise leaders of the nation*: this probably refers to the early hasidic party, the forebears of the later Pharisees, who refused to compromise. At first, they followed a policy of passive resistance (cp. 1 Macc. 2: 29–38). They were thus distinct from the Maccabees, named after Judas Maccabaeus, who were ready to modify the rule about the sabbath, if they were attacked (cp. 1 Macc. 2: 39–41).

34f. *help, though small*: this refers to the rising of the Maccabees. The writer is more impressed by the loyalty of those whose witness ended in death and who thus shared in a vicarious atonement for the community. *Yet there will still be an end*: this seems to indicate the death of Antiochus.

36. *he will exalt and magnify himself*: the pious Jew was most appalled by the king's attempt to claim divinity for himself, as his title Epiphanes suggests. This was the final act of blasphemy, and the *time of wrath* or final judgement was felt to be inevitable. He is described in 1 Maccabees as gloating 'over all he had done' (1 Macc. 1: 24).

37f. *the god beloved of women*: the god here described is Tammuz (cp. Ezek. 8: 14). Antiochus had been a hostage in Rome (1 Macc. 1: 10) and so turns to *the god of the citadel* (Jupiter Capitolinus), for whom he built a magnificent temple in Antioch. The king tended to absorb or suppress local and lesser deities. Hence gods like Apollo and Adonis (= Tammuz) were neglected. His chief aim was the unification of his kingdom (cp. 1 Macc. 1: 41–2), but, apart from the Jews, the majority were apparently happier with the identification of their chief divinity with Jupiter whose worship Antiochus was supporting. Besides, non-Jews were accustomed to think of the king as the living representation of the divinity.

39. *He will garrison his strongest fortresses with aliens*: the Jews particularly resented the presence of gentile garrisons in Jerusalem (cp. Dan. 11: 31; 1 Macc. 1: 33-4; 14: 36).

40-3. The attention now passes to the events immediately preceding the establishment of God's rule. We have no historical support for the supposed attack on Egypt. The reference to *Libyans and Cushites* probably indicates that the furthest confines of Egypt are to fall into Antiochus' hands.

44. The *rumours from east and north* which *alarm him* are reminiscent of the story of Sennacherib's retreat from Jerusalem (cp. Isa. 37: 36-8; 2 Kings 19: 35-7).

45. *between the sea and the holy hill... he will meet his end*: the expectation of the writer was influenced by the prophecies which pointed to this area as the site of the final climax to history (cp. Ezek. 38: 14-16; 39: 2-4; Joel 3: 2). In actual fact Antiochus died of an undiagnosed disease at Tabae in Persia. The writer is mistaken about the manner of Antiochus' death, but his conviction that God will be seen to be triumphant is far more important than an ability to prognosticate precise details about the future. ✳

HISTORY REACHES ITS CLIMAX: (4) THE FINAL VICTORY

12   'At that moment Michael shall appear,
             Michael the great captain,
                who stands guard over your fellow-countrymen;
             and there will be a time of distress
             such as has never been
                since they became a nation till that moment.
         But at that moment your people will be delivered,[a]
             every one who is written in the book:

[a] *Or* will escape.

114

many of those who sleep in the dust of the earth will 2
    wake,
    some to everlasting life
and some to the reproach of eternal abhorrence.
The wise leaders shall shine like the bright vault of heaven, 3
    and those who have guided the people in the true path
    shall be like the stars for ever and ever.

But you, Daniel, keep the words secret and seal the book 4
till the time of the end. Many will be at their wits' end,
and punishment will be heavy.'

* With these verses the vision, begun at 10: 1, comes to an
end. Ch. 11 was concerned with human history, but these
four verses move from the sphere of the temporal to the
eternal. With the death of Antiochus Epiphanes the final age
is inaugurated, and, with Michael as her heavenly representative, Israel finds that the point of her greatest anguish is the
point of her exaltation. The new age can only be entered
through suffering. Right is vindicated through the resurrection
of both the righteous and the wicked, each to receive his
reward, and the eternal kingdom of the saints comes into
being. Here the vision ends; the record is to be kept untouched.
    1. *Michael the great captain*: as the future kingdom is seen
as the kingdom of the saints (i.e. the faithful Israelites),
Michael, as Israel's patron angel, is active in the events leading
up to the end. Fundamentally, he is the representative of the
supreme God, who ensures that God's will is accomplished
on earth. He assists in the redemption of Israel at the end of
time (cp. 10: 13, 21). *everyone who is written in the book*: this
suggests that God knows what human destiny is to be (cp.
note on 11: 1). It has been suggested that, originally, there
may have been a link with Babylonian astral religion, according to which one's fate was predetermined by the stars. Here,
however, the *book* speaks of God's unchangeable will and is

the register of those enrolled for eternal life (cp. Ps. 69: 28; Mal. 3: 16). The New Testament also refers to a 'book' (cp. Phil. 4: 3; Rev. 3: 5; N.E.B. 'the roll of the living').

2. *many...who sleep...will wake*: this prediction of the resurrection of individuals is almost unparalleled in the Old Testament. The passage which is closest to it comes from a late section of Isaiah (26: 19). Originally the Hebrews believed in Sheol, 'the place appointed for all mortal men' (Job 30: 23), which was regarded as a shadowy, half-conscious existence, where communion with God is no more and where one is outside the reach of God's mercy (cp. Isa. 38: 18; Ps. 88: 10–12). Gradually there emerged a hope, based first upon the feeling that God would limit the power of death (cp. Isa. 65: 20–2; 25: 8), and then upon the conviction that close fellowship with God is of such a character that death cannot terminate it (cp. Ps. 16: 9–11). The idea of resurrection was first raised in corporate terms, as God's commitment of himself to Israel was seen as the guarantee of the nation's resurrection (cp. Hos. 6: 2; 13: 14; Ezek. 37). Here, however, for the first time, we have resurrection for reward and punishment. It is felt that the faithful who perished as martyrs in the persecution before the inauguration of the new age must participate in it, if God is righteous. Likewise, the wicked who appeared to prosper in this life could only meet their just reward if they, too, were raised from the dead. It is possible that the writer is thinking of apostates who allied themselves with Antiochus Epiphanes in his attempt to establish pagan worship. The author does not yet teach a general resurrection or a final judgement for all men.

3. *The wise leaders shall shine*: The wise (Hebrew *maskilim*) refers to a group which proved itself as teachers and martyrs in the persecution. At Qumran the same word was used as a technical term for instructors in the community. There is a link between *stars* and angels, and it is possible to see a reference to the communion of exalted spirits with the angels.

4. The injunction to *keep the words secret and seal the book*

is necessary, because the message purports to belong to the sixth century B.C., whilst its application belongs to the time of Antiochus Epiphanes, when the book was actually issued. Contrast Rev. 22: 10, where the book is *not* to be sealed, because the time of fulfilment is near to the time of writing. *punishment will be heavy*: the Hebrew has 'knowledge', but a simple emendation gives us the word for *punishment*. If the manuscript reading is correct, we can only suppose that knowledge will be scarce (cp. Amos 8: 11–12). The emended reading suggests something of the challenge before the new age dawns. ✻

HOW LONG, O LORD? HOW LONG?

And I, Daniel, looked and saw two others standing, 5 one on this bank of the river and the other on the opposite bank. And I[a] said to the man clothed in linen who was 6 above the waters of the river, 'How long will it be before these portents cease?' The man clothed in linen above the 7 waters lifted to heaven his right hand and his left, and I heard him swear by him who lives for ever: 'It shall be for a time, times, and a half. When the power of the holy people ceases to be dispersed, all these things shall come to an end.' I heard but I did not understand, and so I 8 said, 'Sir, what will the issue of these things be?' He 9 replied, 'Go your way, Daniel, for the words are kept secret and sealed till the time of the end. Many shall 10 purify themselves and be refined, making themselves shining white, but the wicked shall continue in wickedness and none of them shall understand; only the wise leaders shall understand. From the time when the regular 11 offering is abolished and "the abomination of desolation"

[a] *So Sept.; Heb.* he.

is set up, there shall be an interval of one thousand two
12 hundred and ninety days. Happy the man who waits and
lives to see the completion of one thousand three hundred
13 and thirty-five days! But go your way to the end and
rest, and you shall arise to your destiny at the end of the
age.'

✻ The heart of the message has already been delivered, and
these verses are little more than an epilogue which attempts
to fix the time of the end. Two further angels appear (verse 5),
perhaps to witness the oath which 'the man clothed in linen'
(verse 7) is to swear, assuring Daniel that the time of severe
persecution will last for three and a half years, as in 7: 25.
Daniel seeks for further illumination, but this is not granted. In
place of the 1150 days (cp. 8: 14) we have successive changes to
1290 and 1335 days (12: 11f.), but whether these are glosses or
not is unclear. If they are interpolations, it is not easy to
visualize a situation in which such slight modifications of the
original figure could have been added. The book ends with
Daniel's death and resurrection foretold. He is to have his
share in the new era.

5. *two others*: Deut. 19: 15 requires two witnesses for
an oath (cp. 8: 13–16, where there are only two involved
besides Daniel).

7. *swear by him who lives for ever*: the eternity of God is the
surety for the continuing truth of what is affirmed (cp. Rev.
10: 5–6).

*When the power of the holy people ceases to be dispersed, all these
things shall come to an end*: some commentators emend the
text to 'the power of the shatterer of the holy people...',
taking this to be a reference to Antiochus Epiphanes as the
last persecutor before the end comes. The N.E.B. translation
is less specific, but still suggests the end of persecution.

10. For the idea of a final separation of the righteous and
wicked cp. Rev. 22: 11.

11f. The majority of commentators take these verses as successive glosses which seek to prolong the time of waiting. Some suppose that the author added the first gloss, when the 1150 days had passed and nothing happened, and that another hand added the second. The first correction to 1290 days may be an attempt to give the longest period for three and a half years. The addition of another 45 days could perhaps have been intended to provide further time for the establishment of the new kingdom *after* the death of Antiochus and the rededication of the temple to the worship of Yahweh. ✶

✶ ✶ ✶ ✶ ✶ ✶ ✶ ✶ ✶ ✶ ✶ ✶ ✶

THE MESSAGE OF THE BOOK

We have seen that, despite its use of symbolism and cryptic numbers, the book of Daniel is not to be treated as a piece of writing through whose magical guidelines we can predict the future. Although the revelation is given to the wise, its message was basically a contemporary one. It was dealing not with an imaginary, but a real situation. Accordingly, we can see the book telling us something about the life of faith.

The writer of the Letter to Hebrews says that 'Faith gives substance to our hopes, and makes us certain of realities we do not see' (Heb. 11: 1). Paul, too, suggests that there is a sense in which what is not seen and yet is grasped in faith has a greater measure of reality and permanence than what is seen (2 Cor. 4: 18). So the book of Daniel, like the book of Revelation, also written in an age of persecution, asserts that the unseen reality can challenge all appearances. Appearance is only transient. The empires come and go. They may be powerful and fearful, but their destruction is seen as inevitable. The abiding reality is God himself, and God is concerned with this world. He is represented as having his plan and purpose for the world, a plan and purpose which are universal in their scope, embracing all nations. In place of Babylon, Media, Persia and Greece, the empires which cannot endure, the divine kingdom issues from heaven. The 'kingdom' is not a human achievement; it is a gift of God. Daniel speaks of the kingly authority as bestowed upon the heavenly man (Dan. 7: 13), but he is the heavenly representative of a larger group, the 'saints of the Most High' (7: 18, 25) who share in his royal dominion. Men of faith can therefore hold on to the assurance that, though their testing may become even more horrific, the issue is certain. Faith looks beyond the fires of persecution – even beyond death itself – to the gift of resurrection (12: 3). 'Have no fear, little flock; for your Father has chosen to give you the Kingdom' (Luke 12: 32).

But the assurance that God has a plan means that the faithful can have a purpose in life. The men of faith can live in hope, and through their hope they also express their belief in change and their rejection of a fatalistic acceptance of the situation as it is. For men without hope the succession of bestial rules and the ever-increasing tempo of persecution would lead to the paralysed inactivity we associate with despair. Hope, in terms of the message of Daniel, speaks of a God who transforms all things and enables the faithful 'to laugh at impossibilities and to say: "It shall be done!"' The man who lives in hope is no longer confined; he sees that world dominion belongs to him. True humanity does not come from the sea of chaos (7: 3–7), but from the presence of God, and in the kingdom, where the truly human one reigns, man's likeness to God will also be fulfilled. That is why the 'wise leaders shall shine like the bright vault of heaven' (12: 3). The book is raising the clarion call: 'Lift up your hearts!' It also provides the reply of the men of faith, who live in hope: 'We lift them up to the Lord.'

Further, the book speaks of loyalty and obedience, which are the way in which faith and hope manifest themselves. Loyalty to God and the revelation of his will and purpose mean that there is to be no compromise with values or patterns of life opposed to God, no matter what the consequences may be. Here is seen the basis of a true heroism. All accommodation to other ideologies is rejected. This does not lead to an exclusivism which means that one opts out of responsibility for this world. Daniel is seen as a faithful servant of gentile kings, ready to use his divinely-given powers in the service of the state. What is rejected is an easy-going attitude, which flings all thought of principle to the winds. The man of loyalty will not fall into the materialistic trap – the service of Mammon in place of the service of God.

The demand for obedience to God is also seen as absolute. There is no promise of immediate reward; there is no specially packaged security. The risk is still there. Obedience to God can mean suffering or social ostracism. The faithful call to God, and yet God seems to tarry. The persecution gets fiercer and fiercer; it is as though some are mocking at the divine authority itself. But here the obedient (the *Hasidim* – the *loyal* ones who have committed themselves to God and who wish to live in accordance with his will) are reminded that God has not abdicated his control. What he wills to endure alone will endure. There is a clear allusion to the message of the book of Daniel, when Jesus says to his disciples: 'You are the men who have stood firmly by me in my times of trial; and now I vest in you the kingship which my Father vested in me; you shall eat and drink at my table in my kingdom and sit on thrones as judges of the twelve tribes of Israel' (Luke 22: 28–30). 'We shall overcome...' is the song of those who live by this vision.

A NOTE ON FURTHER READING

A brief survey of the background, historical and religious, is to be found in D. S. Russell, *The Jews from Alexander to Herod*, New Clarendon Bible (O.U.P., 1967). A much more detailed study of the history appears in the two-volume work of E. R. Bevan, *The House of Seleucus*, new ed. (Routledge and Kegan Paul, 1966). For the religious background and, in particular, for an understanding of apocalyptic, the following, though far from easy reading, may be consulted: M. Hengel, *Judaism and Hellenism* (S.C.M., 1974); K. Koch, *The Rediscovery of Apocalyptic* (S.C.M., 1972); O. Plöger, *Theocracy and Eschatology* (Basil Blackwell, 1968); H. H. Rowley, *The Relevance of Apocalyptic*, 2nd ed. (Lutterworth Press, 1947); D. S. Russell, *The Method and Message of Jewish Apocalyptic* (S.C.M., 1964). Of the many commentaries on the book of Daniel the general reader will find most help in E. W. Heaton, *The Book of Daniel* (S.C.M., 1956); A. Jeffrey, *The Book of Daniel*, The Interpreter's Bible, vol. VI (Abingdon Press, 1956); N. Porteous, *Daniel*, Old Testament Library (S.C.M., 1965). For detailed textual material reference must be made to R. H. Charles, *A Critical and Exegetical Commentary on the Book of Daniel* (O.U.P., 1929) and to J. A. Montgomery, *The Book of Daniel* (T. & T. Clark, 1927). For the feel of the book A. C. Welch, *Visions of the End* (James Clarke & Co., 1922) can still be consulted with profit. The following commentaries also contain material valuable for the study of the book of Daniel: J. R. Bartlett, *The First and Second Books of the Maccabees*, The Cambridge Bible Commentary (C.U.P., 1973); J. C. Dancy, *The Shorter Books of the Apocrypha*, The Cambridge Bible Commentary (C.U.P., 1972).

INDEX

Abed-nego (companion of Daniel) 3, 20, 38, 39, 44

'abomination of desolation' 86, 99, 113

Adam 78

Adonai, Lord 19

Adonis (= Tammuz) 113

Ahasuerus (Xerxes), king xi, 8, 96, 107, 108

Ahikar, story of 55

Alexander the Great, king xii, 4, 84, 90; conquests of 9, 85, 101, 108; divisions of empire after death of 9–10, 32, 84–5, 90, 108

Alexandria 10

Amos 53

ancient in years 75–7

angelic patrons of the nations 14, 51, 78, 103, 115

angels (watchers) 42, 51, 52, 56, 78, 79, 85, 88, 102, 103, 118

animal imagery 14

Anshan xi, 8

Antigonus 9, 108

Antiochus III the Great, king xii, 10, 33, 109

Antiochus IV Epiphanes, king xii, 6, 8, 10, 12, 44, 76, 96, 101, 107, 110–11; assumption of divine honours 13, 40, 86, 113; character of 7, 13, 38, 110; crisis for Jews in time of 10–12, 74–5, 89–90, 94, 98–9, 117–18; death of 5, 11, 91, 112–13, 114, 115, 119; designated as a 'small horn' 13, 76, 84–5; endeavour to suppress Judaism 4–5, 11, 38–9, 81, 84, 95, 110, 112, 116; God's judgment on 13, 32, 88, 114; hostage in Rome 10, 81, 113; meaning of 'Epiphanes' 13, 113

apocalyptic literature 2, 3, 77, 89; pseudonymous character of 2

Apocrypha 1, 12

apostates, Jewish 42, 113, 116

Aramaic 6, 7, 27, 49, 89

Artaxerxes, king xi, 62

Assyria 9, 31

Babel 18–19

Babylon 8–9, 18–19, 26, 31–2, 39, 49, 84, 96; conquest by Cyrus 4, 9, 21–2

Babylonian Empire 8, 31, 34, 60, 61, 120

bagpipe 5, 40

Bel (Ba'al), god 7, 19, 20, 30, 31, 32, 39, 50, 64

Belshazzar, king xi, 4, 7, 8, 48, 60, 61, 63, 64, 65, 75, 84, 91

Belteshazzar (name given to Daniel) 20, 50, 64, 102

Berosus xi

book of life 77, 115–16

Book of Truth 103

Cambyses xi

canon, formation of 1, 5; divisions of 1

Carchemish 19, 26

Chaldaeans 4, 19, 26, 27, 41

Chronicles, books of 5

conversion 34

crisis (in time of Antiochus IV) 74, 94, 99

Cyrus xi, 4, 8, 9, 21, 22, 49, 64, 84, 101, 107

Cyrus Cylinder 64

Dan'el 3, 50

Daniel 2, 4, 28, 34, 48, 54, 63–5, 68–70, 71–2, 84, 94–5, 118; acknowledges God as source of wisdom 25–7; and his companions 2, 3, 4, 12, 21, 27; associated with Chaldaeans 21, 27, 50, 63; meaning of name 13; receives revelation from God 14, 21, 25, 52–3, 80–1, 88–9, 107; type of the loyal Jew 3, 14, 20, 121

125

INDEX

Nehemiah 4, 69
New Year festival 61, 77, 103

obedience 120–1
Onias III (high priest) 10, 11, 20, 95, 98–9, 110

Persian Empire, Persian period 4, 7, 8, 9, 31, 84, 120
Persian words 5, 19, 28, 40, 69
Plato 51
Polybius (historian) 40, 91
prayer 25, 69–70, 96–8, 102
prophecy (prophets) 12, 13, 14, 97
proselytism 33
Psalms, book of 13
Ptolemies (kings) xii, 10, 20, 33, 85, 108–11
Ptolemy (general of Alexander the Great) xii, 9, 108

Qumran 1, 2, 51, 81, 96–7, 116; *see also* Dead Sea Scrolls

resurrection, belief in 38, 116–17, 118
Revelation, book of 2, 14, 79, 91, 117, 118–19
revelation, reveal 2, 3, 14, 15, 28, 80, 89, 102, 107
Rome 10, 11, 81, 109–11

saints 13, 78, 81
Satraps 9, 68–9
secrets 14, 15, 27, 28, 34, 91, 116–17
Seleucids (kings) xii, 10, 20, 33, 62, 76, 85, 90, 101, 108–11
Seleucus (general of Alexander the Great) xii, 9, 108
Seleucus IV, king xii, 10, 76, 110

Septuagint x, 7, 12, 42, 49, 51, 65, 89, 98
seventy years (of exile) 62, 95–6
Shadrach (companion of Daniel) 3, 20, 38, 39, 44
Sheol 116
Shinar 19
Sibylline oracles 1–2
Solomon, king 26
son of man (human figure) 77–9, 88–9
Song of the Three 7, 42
Susanna 7
symbolism 3, 14, 32, 75, 88, 119
synagogues 33

temple in Jerusalem: destruction 61, 98; desecration 4, 5, 11, 12, 82, 84, 86, 112; rededication 5, 11, 12, 86, 119
Theodotion x, 7, 90
Tiamat 75

Ugaritic literature 3, 77

visions 2, 28, 80, 88–9, 91, 94

watchers *see* angels
weeks of years 95, 98
wisdom 3, 13, 15, 21, 25, 26, 34, 47–8
wisdom literature 26
wise 3, 15, 47, 81, 116, 119–20

Xenophon (historian) 19, 61
Xerxes, king *see* Ahasuerus

Zerubbabel 20, 99
Zeus Olympios (god) 81, 86, 99
Zeus, Ouranios (god) 28

DEC 08 1998	DATE DUE	
JAN 3 0 2001		
APR 2 4 2001		
MAY 0 4 2001		
JUL 0 3 2009		